The Architecture of Language

The Architecture of Language

NOAM CHOMSKY

edited by
Nirmalangshu Mukherji
Bibudhendra Narayan Patnaik
Rama Kant Agnihotri

OXFORD
UNIVERSITY PRESS

OXFORD
UNIVERSITY PRESS

Oxford University Press is a department of the University of Oxford.
It furthers the University's objective of excellence in research, scholarship,
and education by publishing worldwide. Oxford is a registered trademark of
Oxford University Press in the UK and in certain other countries

Published in India by
Oxford University Press
YMCA Library Building, 1 Jai Singh Road, New Delhi 110001, India

First published 2000
Oxford India Paperbacks 2006
Thirteenth impression 2017

ISBN-13: 978-0-19-568446-9
ISBN-10: 0-19-568446-X

Printed in India by Replika Press Pvt. Ltd.

Royalties go to Eklavya, an NGO in Madhya Pradesh, India

Contents

Editors' Preface

Noam Chomsky is one of the most creative and widely published authors on language and mind. Apart from writing many books and papers, he has addressed, and continues to address, a vast range of audiences all over the world on these topics. A number of these lectures have been published in book-form.[1] None the less, we thought that another addition to this large, and growing catalogue was in order.

Chomsky was in India for about a week in January 1996. The visit started with a series of lectures in Delhi.[2] Of the five public lectures he delivered, only one concerned his work on language and mind.[3] The event generated unprecedented enthusiasm in the academic community of Delhi. The lecture itself took about an hour and a half, and was followed by a very vigorous question-and-answer session covering a wide variety of topics. So many questions were submitted, and left unanswered, that Chomsky agreed to respond to these when he returned to MIT. A set of questions was compiled by the Department of Linguistics, Delhi University, and sent to Chomsky. He sent back detailed responses within a month.

We are told that a similar response is generated wherever Noam Chomsky speaks. However, this kind of popular, prolonged and intense intellectual debate is seldom seen in the Indian academic scene. Chomsky was visiting India after a gap of over twenty-five years and, given his busy schedule, there is no telling when—or indeed if—he will return. So the occasion itself, especially the vigorous participation of the audience, was well worth documenting. Moreover, after the event, many requests were received for copies of the recording and transcripts of the proceedings. Many eager enquirers to whom Chomsky generously replied from MIT were lost to the organizers once the audience had dispersed; and we felt a responsibility to at least attempt to reach them. Hence this book.

There is also a purely intellectual reason for publishing this volume. Chomsky was given the arduous task of tracing the entire historical chain of events, which began with his early research on language[4] and led up to the Minimalist Program (Chomsky 1995b). He was also requested to sketch some of the key technical innovations that have characterized generative grammar in recent years. Thus it was meant to be a general public lecture as well as a technical address to professional linguists.

Readers will judge for themselves how well this task has been accomplished by Chomsky. Yet the fact that this task was even attempted was astounding. We do not know of any recent, published material where he covered this much ground within the span of a single lecture. As far as we know, his published lectures—sometimes a series of them—usually cover either general and philosophical issues with a very informal discussion on his technical work,[5] or they delve straight into a technical discussion after brief preliminary remarks of a general nature. In this lecture he covered both, and he did it not just to oblige the hosts, as the careful organization of the lecture shows. We feel that in this lecture he made an attempt to achieve a prolificacy that is fast becoming unattainable.

It often happens in the history of science that the general conceptual goals of a research programme are only marginally realized in the actual technical work. One may entertain a large body of philosophical, methodological, and commonsensical arguments to urge some conceptual points; but empirical research continues for a long time virtually unhindered by these arguments. Keeping to contemporary linguistics, one recalls that although the characterization of Universal Grammar as a genetic endowment was the stated goal of contemporary linguistics almost from its inception,[6] for the most part empirical research had indeed very little to contribute simply because the design principles of Universal Grammar were largely unknown in their operating detail. As Chomsky notes in the lecture, the first major breakthrough took place with the principles and parameters framework in the early eighties, when the concept began to be realized in terms of concrete empirical research.

This inevitably forced a certain change in the style and content of Chomsky's subsequent presentations, including his writings. For example, in the book *Knowledge of Language* (1986),[7] Chomsky devoted a much larger part (in fact, the major part) to fairly technical discussions which had animated linguistic research for years. The stage had arrived where general philosophical points could be probed in-depth with real and subtle empirical evidence and novel technical tools.[8] Even then it was largely possible for the general reader to get a flavour of the discipline while ignoring the technical parts. It was also possible for professional linguists to ignore the 'philosophical' chapters without losing the momentum of the argument. Each of these moves was, however, becoming increasingly untenable.

The principles and parameters framework brought the principles of Universal Grammar and language faculty to the centre stage of linguistic research.[9] As some of the unexpected and deep properties of this faculty began to surface, one could raise questions that were unimaginable just a few years ago. How exactly is the part of the mind designed for the purposes of language acquisition given the conditions in which language acquisition takes place? What part of the theory captures this design and what part merely displays theoretical convenience? In what sense is the language faculty a *biological* system? It is extraordinary that these questions can in fact be raised and, in part, pursued within rigorous empirical research. A large body of general, conceptual, empirical and technical concerns thus converge within one programme.[10] Chances are that one is likely to miss something terribly important about the whole programme if one misses any one of these individual parts. This applies not only to the general reader, but may well include professional linguists. Thus the urgency of the task increases as the task itself gets more difficult.

The present lecture, in our view, was an occasion in which Chomsky made an attempt to accomplish the task of integrating philosophical and conceptual issues on the one hand and technical innovations and empirical research on the other. He covered the entire history of generative grammar, picking just those points which ultimately led to the Minimalist Program. Along the way, he spelt out the assumptions about the cognitive systems in which the current research on the architecture of the language faculty is embedded, and provided indications regarding the direction this research may take. In the process, many old questions were rephrased, many issues which occupied centre stage earlier were side-stepped or even dismissed, and the bare logic of the new programme displayed with amazing sophistication and clarity. Those interested in the internal history of modern generative linguistics will find the lecture immensely insightful.

Not surprisingly, questions came from all parts of the audience, including professional linguists. Chomsky's patient and extended responses clarified many points that he had barely touched upon during the lecture. The lecture and the responses, thus, together form an accessible whole in which much of the salient features of the new programme find clear articulation.

As noted, some of the questions were answered during the session itself, while the rest were answered in writing from MIT. In the excitement (and the resulting confusion) of the event, it turned out that Chomsky actually responded in writing to some questions that he had already answered during the session. As such, several questions had dual answers—verbal and written. Sometimes these answers differed substantially in style and content, but for the purposes of this volume, we have tried our best to include both responses within a single, coherent text. We leave it to the reader to locate these 'mixed' answers; we will feel rewarded if they cannot find them.

As for the organization of the discussion, we took advantage of the fact that the questions were submitted in writing, and were therefore not answered in any particular order. Despite the variety, the questions largely belonged to three groups which seemed to correspond to the three major parts of the talk. The questions are arranged here accordingly in decreasing order of generality within each group: the scope of linguistics, acquisition of language, and theory of language.

We have also added some clarificatory notes and references for those who might wish to pursue the issues further. Moreover, as the reader will see, Chomsky felt constrained to narrow his audience when he dealt with the cutting edge of the discipline. The extended notes provided here, written, in what we hope is a somewhat more accessible style, will enable at least some of the general readers to get a feel for the technical points.[11] Since Chomsky was unable to look at much of the added material, we assume full responsibility for these sections.

The task was distributed among the three of us as follows. Mukherji and Patnaik transcribed the material initially.[12] Mukherji wrote the draft of this preface, and prepared an early list of notes and references. Patnaik wrote the technical notes and added some further notes and references. Agnihotri looked at the prepared material at each stage and suggested changes; he also oversaw the project, acting as a liaison between Mukherji, Patnaik, Chomsky and the publishers. Each of us repeatedly checked one's reservations with the others. This little volume is truly a result of a friendly and co-operative venture, which Noam Chomsky made possible.

We wish to express our thanks to the Department of Linguistics, Delhi University, for sponsoring the project; to the Indian Institute of Advanced Study, Shimla for facilitating the preparation of the material. We thank Professor A.K. Sinha for his help and encouragement. Special thanks to Tista Bagchi for collecting and compiling the questions that were sent to Chomsky. Finally, our sincerest thanks to Noam Chomsky himself for taking such an active interest in the project.

N. Mukherji
B.N. Patnaik
R.K. Agnihotri

NOTES

[1] See Chomsky (1987a, 1987b, 1988, 1993a, etc.).

[2] From Delhi Chomsky went to Calcutta, Hyderabad, Trivandrum, Mysore and Bombay.

[3] Delivered at the Tagore Hall, Delhi University. The other lectures were on political issues and were delivered at the Delhi School of Economics (twice), Jawaharlal Nehru University and at the Shankarlal Hall, Delhi University.

[4] See Chomsky (1955), which is a partially modified version of a manuscript that includes his Ph.D. thesis, submitted to the University of Pennsylvania. However, Chomsky (1957), and its subsequent review by Robert Lee (1957) in *Language*, catapulted Chomsky to international fame. Among non-linguists, Chomsky's recognition may be traced to his 1959 review of B. F. Skinner's *Verbal Behaviour* (see Katz and Fodor 1964). The 1975 debate between Chomsky and Piaget (reported in Piattelli-Palmarini 1980) is another landmark in Chomsky's international recognition. See Barsky (1997) for a description of some of these and other significant events in Chomsky's career. See also Chomsky et al. (1982). Some of these events are also captured in the film *Manufacturing Consent: Noam Chomsky and the Media*, by Peter Wintonick and Mark Achbar, Montreal.

[5] These include the items cited in note 1.

[6] See Chomsky (1965, especially chapter 1) for a clear and explicit statement of this goal.

[7] See Chomsky (1986a).

[8] Chomsky has written three types of monographs on language and mind: (a) purely technical ones addressed to professional linguists (1955, 1965, 1981, 1982, 1986b, 1995b etc.), (b) general ones meant for the non-professional larger audience (1987a, 1987b, 1988, 1993a, 1997 etc.), and (c) fairly technical ones addressed to professionals in adjacent fields and linguists alike (1966, 1972a, 1975, 1980, 1986a). As George (1987: 155) puts it, items in (c) typically included '. . . articulation of the general framework within which Chomsky sees the project of linguistics, glimpses of the

details of the current theory, and by-now familiar 'take on all comers' section in which Chomsky attempts to neutralise any perceived challenge to the enterprise, especially those coming from philosophical quarters'. Chomsky has not published anything of that scope since his (1986a). In our view, the present lecture does not really belong to the category of material in (a) or (b). Although the material presented here is much smaller in length and scope than those listed in (c), we think that it belongs essentially to the same category.

⁹ See Jan Koster, Henk van Riemsdijk and Jean-Roger Vernaud, 'The GLOW Manifesto' (in Carlos Otero (ed.), 1994, Vol. 1, p. 342). 'GLOW' stands for 'Generative Linguists in the Old World', an international organization based in Europe.

¹⁰ One is naturally tempted to draw analogies with more illuminating parts of the history of science, but the exercise is best left to the reader. There are some hints from Chomsky on this point in the discussion.

¹¹ The technical notions clarified in the notes are in terms of some earlier versions of the principles and parameters framework; at certain places, some broad hints have been given as to how some of these notions have been altered or dispensed within the later versions.

¹² Transcribing the lecture and the discussion created familiar problems:

> Part of the problem comes from the circumstances of transcription: the intonation and timing that delineate phrases is lost, and a transcription from anything but the highest-fidelity tape is unreliable. Indeed, in the White House's independent transcription of ... low-quality recording, many puzzling passages are rendered more sensibly. For example, *I want the, uh, uh, to go* is transcribed as *I want them, uh, uh, to go*. (Pinker 1995: 224)

We did not even use *high*-fidelity tapes. Thus, first, we deleted the *uh, uh*s and reconstructed the *them*s to which punctuation marks, paragraphs etc. were added. Next, after several rounds of style-editing, a draft, along with a series of suggestions, was sent to Chomsky. Chomsky made a very large number of corrections, modifications, additions and deletions. These were incorporated in the text before the final 'copy-editing'.

Language and its Design

THE DELHI LECTURE, JANUARY 1996

I am torn by two temptations. One is to talk about the interesting set of questions that were just raised.[1] The other is to talk about the topic that I was asked to talk about which is a rather different one. I'd like to talk about the questions that Professor Agnihotri just raised, but perhaps it would be best to put that off until the discussion.

Can you hear me? Probably you can't hear me.

(Section of the audience): No.

If you say 'no', then you can.

The short answer to the question of the relation between the two topics is that, yes indeed, I am interested in both. One concerns language as a biological organ—it is pretty clear that it is—and this, I think, gives quite a lot of insight into the essential nature of human beings. The other topic concerns human life and its problems and the use of language as a technique of exploitation and so on. But in that second domain there is nothing known of any depth, to my knowledge. People may pretend that there is and they may make it look complicated; that is the job of intellectuals. But the fact of the matter is that what is understood is pretty much on the surface and is easily available anyway.

Science is a very strange activity. It only works for simple problems. Even in the hard sciences, when you move beyond the simplest structures, it becomes very descriptive. By the time you get to big molecules, for example, you are mostly describing things. The idea that deep scientific analysis tells you something about problems of human beings and our lives and our inter-relations with one another and so on is mostly pretence in my opinion—self-serving pretence which is itself a technique of domination and exploitation and should be avoided. Professionals certainly have the responsibility of not making people believe that they have some special knowledge that others can't attain without special means or special college education or whatever. If things are simple, they should be said simply; if there is something serious to say that is not simple, then, fine, that's good and interesting. We can perhaps find deep answers to certain questions that do bear directly on issues of human interest and concern, but that is rarely true. Anyhow, that is my opinion. So I am interested in both topics[2] and spend a great deal of time and effort on both, but they just don't seem to merge.

Let me talk about the area where surprisingly the approach of rational enquiry (that is, the approach of natural sciences) actually seems to get somewhere in the study of complex organisms, namely in the area of human language. This is one of the very few areas of complex human functioning where we can apparently find surprising, and maybe even rather deep, things of the kind that you can find by studying few other aspects of the natural world. There aren't many but there are some and this appears to be one of them, or so I hope.

What I'd like to do is to outline some recent phases of a programme of research that goes back a long time. I want to lead up to things that have been happening in the last few years in what's come to be called the 'Minimalist Program'. I will mention something about its background assumptions and motivations, some of the directions that have been pursued and the relevance of all of this to classical questions of enquiry into mind and language. I will only be able to barely touch on the last topic; I could go on with it if you like since these questions are still very much alive. The linguistic work itself gets pretty technical very fast but I'll just keep to general outlines. But again, if you like, I'll pursue some of the more technical parts.

First, just some of the background assumptions. They are fairly familiar and I think that they are adopted much more widely than many people believe. I don't think they are specific to this programme. They are usually tacitly adopted but if we are trying to pursue the topic seriously we better make explicit what is tacitly assumed. To say that they are common and familiar is not to say that they should be adopted uncritically; that is far from true. When you think about these assumptions, they are pretty surprising in many respects and hence interesting, to the extent that they are at all plausible on empirical grounds.

The first one is the assumption that there is a language faculty, that is, there is some part of the mind–brain, which is dedicated to the knowledge and use of language. That is a particular function in the body; it is a kind of language organ, roughly analogous to the visual system which is also dedicated to a particular task. Now, that is an assumption but there is good evidence that it is true.

Furthermore, there is good evidence that it is an actual species property in two senses. First of all, there appears to be very little variation across the species, apart from really serious pathology. Over quite a broad range, the basic properties of the faculty seem close to identical. In that respect it is not unlike the visual system. However, it is unlike the human visual system in another respect in which it is a species property:[3] namely, it is apparently unique to the species. There does not seem to be anything homologous (that is, biologically related) or even analogous, which is a weaker property, in other related species.

If you want to find similarities to the properties of the language faculty in the animal world you can find some though they are pretty remote; but it is interesting that the most similar systems are found in insects or in birds where there is no common evolutionary origin at all as far as language is concerned. But if you get to organisms where there is relevantly common evolutionary origin, say the primates, there is simply nothing with interesting similarities, which means that the language faculty appears to be biologically isolated in a curious and unexpected sense.

To tell a fairy tale about it, it is almost as if there was some higher primate wandering around a long time ago and some random mutation took place, maybe after some strange cosmic ray shower, and it reorganized the brain, implanting a language organ in an otherwise primate brain. That is a story, not to be taken literally. But it may be closer to reality than many other fairy tales that are told about evolutionary processes, including language.

Let us assume then that there is a language faculty and that this faculty includes at least a cognitive system, that is, a system that stores information. There have to be systems that access that information, the performance systems. Now, a factual question arises: to what extent are the systems that access the information stored in the language faculty part of the language faculty? That is, to what extent are the performance systems language-dedicated themselves? Take, say, the sensorimotor systems, the articulatory-perceptual systems which access information that is given to them by the language faculty. Are they themselves part of the language faculty? Are they themselves language-dedicated? That is not really known. The assumption is that, probably, they are dedicated to some extent, and to some extent they are not. But that is a research question—a hard one even at the level of sensorimotor processes and there certainly are other more obscure processes. To some extent at least, the performance systems seem to be part of the language faculty.

Another factual question about the performance systems is whether they change. Are they fixed and invariant? Or do they themselves grow? There is a lot of talk about a language acquisition device, but notice that it is focused on the cognitive system of the language faculty. That one certainly changes. The information that is stored in the language faculty changes through life; a speaker of Hindi is not a speaker of English. So something has changed from a common state. Have the performance systems changed? No one knows much about that, though interesting and difficult questions arise when one investigates the matter more closely. Actual linguistic work often makes the tacit simplifying assumption that these matters do not affect the study of language and particular languages. This would be very strange if it were true; so it is probably false. It is assumed out of ignorance; we do not know that it is false. When you do not know something you make the simplest assumption. The simplest assumption is that it is true although we cannot be confident about that. Sooner or later we may discover that growth of the performance systems has to be integrated more closely into the investigation of the cognitive system of the language faculty, but at the moment we do not know about that. So we put it aside.

We now focus attention on what we *can* look at—namely the cognitive system of the language faculty which certainly does change state. Its common initial genetically determined state is not identical with the states it assumes under different conditions, either because of internal maturational processes or certainly because of external experience. That is what we call 'language acquisition'. It is also called 'learning' but that is a pretty misleading term because it seems more like growth processes than anything that is properly called 'learning'. You put a child in a situation where the right stimulation is around and acquisition of language is something that happens to the child. The child doesn't do anything; it is just like growing when you have food. So it looks like a growth process, rather like the development of the visual system which also can assume different states depending on experience.

We can be pretty confident that the different states that are attained by the language faculty are only different in a superficial fashion and that each one is largely determined by the common language faculty. The reason for believing that is pretty straightforward. It is simply that relevant experience is far too limited. We can check the experience available; we can look at it and see what it is. It is immediately obvious that it is much too limited and fragmentary to do anything more than shape an already existing common form in limited fashions.[4]

Incidentally, it is interesting that this conclusion is considered very controversial in the case of mental faculties, though the same conclusion is considered obvious and trivial in the case of all other growth processes. Take any other growth process, say the fact that an embryo grows arms, not wings, or, to take a post-natal example, that people undergo puberty at a certain age. If someone were to propose that it is the result of experience, people will just laugh. So, if someone were to propose that a child undergoes puberty because of, say, peer pressure ('Others are doing it, I'll do it too.'), people would regard that as ridiculous. But it is no more ridiculous than the belief that the growth of language is a result of experience.

In fact, it is in a way less ridiculous. Nothing much is known about what gets an organism to develop, say, arms or wings or undergo puberty at a certain age, or, for that matter, to die at (roughly) a certain age. Those are all genetically determined properties but ones that are not well understood. But it is always assumed that they are genetically determined and all research in biology just takes that for granted, for a very good reason. If you look at the environmental conditions under which growth takes place, there is simply not enough information there to direct a highly specific, closely articulated uniform process. So, therefore, you assume, angels aside, that it is inner-directed.

Exactly the same argument holds for mental faculties. The fact that people don't accept the argument is due to the residues of a sort of irrational form of dualism which one ought to overcome. In fact in the case of language, we even know something about the properties of the mental state. So in a way, here we are better off than arms and wings and puberty and so on. That is the basic set of assumptions.

We can take a language to be nothing other than a state of the language faculty. That is about as close a concept as the theoretical enquiry into language gives to you, to the intuitive concept of language.[5] So let's take a language to be (say, Hindi or English or Swahili) a particular state attained by the language faculty. And to say that somebody knows a language, or has a language, is simply to say that their language faculty is in that state. The language, in that sense, provides instructions to the performance systems.

The next question is: how does it do it? There is another assumption that comes along: it does it in the form of what are called 'linguistic expressions'. Each linguistic expression is some collection of properties. The technical terminology for that is that the language generates an infinite set of expressions; that is why the theory of a language is called a 'generative grammar'.[6] It is commonly assumed that the performance systems fall into just two categories which access two different kinds of information: roughly, sound and meaning. You have some kind of representations of sound, some kind of representations of meaning. This assumption goes back thousands of years; now we have to make it more explicit. The representations of sound are accessed by the sensorimotor systems and the representations of meaning (we have to clarify what that means), use the information and the expression to talk about the world, to ask questions, express thoughts and feelings, and so on.

The systems that access representations of meaning can be called 'conceptual-intentional' systems, where 'intentional' is the traditional philosophical term for this mysterious relation of 'aboutness': things are about something. So conceptual-intentional systems, which are mostly mysterious, are the systems that access certain aspects of expressions to enable you to do the things you do with language: express your thoughts, talk about the world, whatever it may be.

Now the assumption that there are just two access systems, two performance systems, is again surprising. It has been assumed without much question since the origin of the study of language thousands of years ago, usually implicitly, without any specific attention. But if you want to pursue the topic seriously, you have to bring it to the surface and when you do so, you notice that it is a very strange assumption. In fact we even know that it is false. From the existence of sign language we know that systems other than the standard articulatory-perceptual systems, can access the information of the language faculty. So it cannot really be true in the sense in which it is usually assumed. But, again, it is assumed to be true because you do not really know that it is radically false and I will continue to assume it here.

So there are sensorimotor systems that access one aspect of an expression and there are conceptual-intentional systems that access another aspect of an expression, which means that an expression has to have two kinds of symbolic objects as its parts. These objects can be regarded as a kind of an interface between the language faculty and other systems of the mind–brain. At this point, we are already into pretty far-reaching empirical assumptions about the architecture of the mind but they seem reasonably plausible and a good basis for continuing.

This much by way of background. You have the foundations for a programme of serious empirical enquiry: try to discover the principles and structures of the language organ, try to figure out what kind of states it can assume (that is, particular languages), what are the expressions that language generates and how are these expressions accessed and used by various performance systems.

Those are all sub-parts of a broad field of empirical enquiry, many parts of which have been opened up for research in new ways in the last forty or fifty years. There are parts we know something about, and parts we do not. I think the study itself is rather similar to the study of the visual system, about which you can ask similar questions. For that matter, it is rather similar, you might say, to chemistry, which tries to figure out what the building blocks of the world are, what their structures and governing principles are, and so on. It has the form of a normal part of the natural sciences. It is unusual because it happens to be about human mental faculties, which are for the most part beyond the level of serious study. This one oddly does not seem to be beyond that level; that is a part of its interest.

At this point, basic questions about the whole enterprise arise; questions about, roughly speaking, how language relates to other aspects of the world. This is one aspect of the world, the language organ: how does it relate to the other aspects of the world?

Now, these questions are quite deeply rooted in at least the western intellectual tradition (I'll keep to that because of my own limitations). These are also very lively topics of contemporary philosophy. They usually take two forms. One form is the question (what's roughly called the question of materialism or physicalism or the mind–body problem or whatever): how can the properties of the language faculty be realized in the physical world? The second form they take is a question which is usually called the question of representation or intentionality ('aboutness'):

the question of how expressions represent reality, how words refer to things. That is the second aspect of the question of the relation between language and the world.

Now, in my opinion, both these questions are radically misconceived, and have been for a long time. There's a lot to say about it, which bears on contemporary philosophy of mind as well as traditional ideas. I don't think there is any intelligible and coherent mind–body question; I don't think there's been one since Newton at least. And the question of representation is based on faulty analogies, I think.[7] Anyhow, I'll come back to that if you like. I'll put it aside by just saying that that's the kind of framework in the intellectual tradition into which much of the research falls.

Let me return to the narrower question (because there is not much time) of the enquiry into the language organ. Take those assumptions that I mentioned. About forty years ago, at the origins of modern generative grammar, problems within this range began to be examined in a far more serious way than had ever been possible in the past, partly because of advances in the formal sciences. There is a crucial property of language which had been grasped intuitively for a long time. In one classical formulation, it was said that language involves infinite use of finite means; that is, the mind is obviously finite but there is an infinite number of expressions that every person can master and use.

Those are obvious facts and the question is: how can you have infinite use of finite means? There never was really any clear general answer to that question until early in this century. By mid-century, the theory of computability and various other achievements finally led to a very precise answer to at least some aspects of the question.

That made it possible to return to the old questions and give them a sharp enough form so that you could try to answer them. It was a kind of confluence of traditional issues in the study of language with new advances in the formal sciences that clarified the basic ideas. Those things coming together made it possible to open up the domain of generative grammar.

It quickly became clear that there was a big problem. As soon as the enquiry into generative grammar began, a conflict arose between two kinds of empirical requirements. One of the requirements came to be called 'descriptive adequacy': you want to give an accurate account of the phenomena of English, Hindi, etc. It immediately became obvious, as soon as serious enquiry was undertaken, that the most comprehensive grammars and dictionaries— *Oxford English Dictionary*, ten-volume grammar of English and so on—were skimming the surface.[8] They only included hints that an intelligent person could somehow use to get information about the language. They were thought to be descriptions of the language but they simply weren't; they were much too superficial. As soon as an effort was made to give a precise articulation of what the actual properties of the expressions were, it was quickly discovered that, even for very simple constructions in the best-studied languages, an awful lot was simply unknown and was never even noticed.

In order to try to deal with that problem it seemed to be necessary to postulate extremely complex mechanisms with varied grammatical constructions, with different properties internal to the language and certainly across languages. The empirical evidence for that was overwhelming but it was also obvious that the conclusion could not be correct.

The conclusion could not be correct because of the second kind of empirical condition that came to be called the 'condition of explanatory adequacy': the problem of accounting for language acquisition.[9] If languages really are that complex and varied and the information available to the language learner is so slight (of course, people aren't genetically adapted to one language or another), then language acquisition becomes a miracle. And it is not a miracle; it is just some natural, organic process. So the conclusion about the variety and complexity of languages cannot be correct although the facts were forcing you in that direction. In other words, languages must somehow be extremely simple and very much like one another; otherwise, you couldn't acquire any of them. Nevertheless, when you looked at them, it turned out that they were extremely complex, very varied and all different from one another.

That looks like a flat contradiction. At the very least it is a serious tension and, from roughly 1960, it was the driving issue in the field to try to resolve that tension somehow. I won't run through the history, but the general approach, starting from the early sixties, was the natural one: try to abstract general principles and properties of rule systems, take them to be properties of the language faculty itself (of language as such, in other words) and try to show that when you do so, the residue, what is left when you've done that, is much less complex and varied than it looks. From the early sixties, there were various attempts to do this; those of you in the field know what they were, I won't bother talking about them.[10]

Anyhow, over about twenty years, various attempts were made and there was a lot of progress. A lot of this work converged around 1980 in an approach which is sometimes called the 'principles and parameters approach', which all of a sudden made sense. It was a radical departure from the tradition of several thousand years of linguistic research. It was far more of a break with the tradition than generative grammar itself was.[11] Generative grammar itself was quite different from the prevailing structuralist-behavioural approaches of the time but it had very much the flavour of traditional grammar; it looked like a refined form of traditional grammar in many ways.

On the other hand, the principles and parameters approach was totally different. It assumed that there are no rules at all and there are no grammatical constructions at all. So, there's nothing like rules for relative clauses in Japanese or rules for verb phrases in German, and so on. Those things are real but as taxonomic artefacts—in the sense in which, say, terrestrial animals are real. It is not a biological category, it is just a taxonomic category. It seems as if rules and grammatical constructions—the core properties of traditional grammar carried over to generative grammar—are taxonomic artefacts in the same sense.

What there *is*, it seems, is just general principles which are properties of the language faculty as such and slight options of variation, which are called 'parameters'. The principles hold across languages and across constructions. So there aren't any special principles for relative clauses or any other constructions. The parametric variations seem to be a finite space, which means that, if true, there are only a finite number of possible languages that satisfy them. Furthermore, they seem to be limited to certain small parts of the language: some parts of the lexicon and certain peripheral aspects of the sensorimotor interface. One hopes to show that these things are easily detectable from the data of experience.

Now this principles and parameters approach is not a

specific theory; it is a kind of theoretical framework, it is a way of thinking about language and it is the first one ever that at least has the right general character; that is, it proposes a way to resolve the tension between explanatory and descriptive adequacy. It would resolve the tension if you could show that the principles which are uniform suffice to give you the general character of the language and the apparent, superficial variations come from just fixing these parameters one way or another within a small range.

It is as if the child comes to the problem of language acquisition with a questionnaire saying 'here's X number of questions I need an answer to' and each of these questions can be answered on the basis of very simple data. When I plug in the answers and I use the principles, which reflect part of my nature, out comes Japanese—something like that.[12] It may look on the surface as if languages are radically different from one another, but that is because you don't know the principles. When you discover the principles, you see that they are really quite the same and that the differences among them are quite superficial.

That is the sort of picture that emerged. It led to a real explosion of research, and a great increase in the amount of descriptive and theoretical work. By now it included quite a wide typologically varied range of languages. It is all very much in flux, I should say, but I don't think there has been a period in the history of the study of language when so much was learnt about it.

It also became possible to raise new and somewhat more principled questions about the nature of language. That is where this work on the Minimalist Program comes along. The point is that you now, for the first time ever, have some coherent idea of what a language might be.[13] Then you can ask certain novel questions.

One question you can ask is how much of what we are attributing to the language faculty is really motivated by empirical evidence and how much by the kind of technology which we adopt because we want to cover gaps of understanding and to present data in a useful form. Now questions like that are always appropriate in principle in the sciences. But they are often not worth proposing or trying to sharpen very closely in practice. The reason is that understanding is just too limited. That is even true in the hard sciences. If you look at their history—in physics, even mathematics, through most of their history until pretty recently, questions of this sort were not raised. Most of classical mathematics, for example, up to the nineteenth century, was based on what were known to be contradictory assumptions; they did not understand enough to resolve the contradictions. People just continued because it led to all sorts of new discoveries, insights, ideas, and so on. The same is true of physics and chemistry. So while these questions are in principle appropriate they are often premature.

One element of the Minimalist Program is the speculation that the questions are now appropriate in practice and in fact can be productively pursued; that is, it is reasonable at this point to ask which parts of the descriptive technology that we use are really empirically motivated and which parts we are using because we are papering over lack of understanding and we need it in order to give a useful account of the data. That question has an answer. Whether this is the time to raise the question or not is unclear but at least in principle the question has an answer.

The Minimalist Program is also based on a further question that might not have an answer even in principle and might be hopelessly premature even if it does have an answer. That question is a more subtle one. It is a question which you could put like this: how good a solution is language to certain boundary conditions that are imposed by the architecture of the mind? The language organ is inserted into a system of mind that has a certain architecture; it has interface relations with that system. It connects to them. The assumption is that there are the two interfaces that I mentioned. Those interfaces impose some conditions on what the system must be like. How good a solution is language to the conditions imposed by those external assumptions?

Let me go back to that fairy tale which I mentioned at the outset about the origin of language. Let us imagine a higher primate wandering around. It lacks the language organ but it has something like our brain and other organs, including sensorimotor systems sufficiently close to ours, and also a conceptual-intentional system sufficiently close to ours so that it can think about the world more or less the way we do in so far as that is possible without language. But it doesn't have language and cannot articulate such thoughts—even to itself.

Suppose some random event causes a language faculty to be installed in that primate and this language faculty is capable of providing an infinity of expressions that can be accessed by the already existing performance systems— say, the sensorimotor and conceptual-intentional systems. To be usable, the expressions of the language faculty (at least some of them), have to be legible by the outside systems. So the sensorimotor system and the conceptual-intentional system have to be able to access, to 'read' the expressions; otherwise the systems wouldn't even know it is there.

In fact it is conceivable, it is an empirical possibility,

though extremely unlikely, that higher primates, say, gorillas or whatever, actually have something like a human language faculty but they just have no access to it. So, too bad, the legibility conditions are not satisfied. Conceivably, what changed in humans is that the language faculty came to meet the legibility conditions. We can safely assume that is not true, and that as the language faculty evolved, it was usable, satisfying external conditions of legibility imposed at the interface.

We can then ask how good a design it is. How well do the laws of nature come to providing an optimal solution to a certain 'engineering problem', namely the engineering problem posed by the legibility conditions on expressions? That is a meaningful question; we can make it fairly concrete, in fact. But there is no reason to expect any interesting answer to it. It could turn out that language is a very bad solution to that problem. That wouldn't be surprising in the least. That is what biological systems usually are; they are bad solutions to certain design problems that are posed by nature—the best solution that evolution could achieve under existing circumstances, but perhaps a clumsy and messy solution.

Let us see what is involved in this. Take any sentence you like, take an old example which is still not very well understood: 'John had a book stolen'. Take that sentence in English. It has lots of empirical properties, including certain very curious multiple ambiguities,[14] which are not matched in similar languages. It is not very well understood why—that is why it is an old chestnut hanging around for about thirty years. The sentence has properties of sound and properties of meaning, multiple ambiguities, sound-meaning correlations—all sorts of things. Quite apart from that, it has lots of other properties. It has properties of order of acquisition, of the loss of various interpretations under brain damage, of perceptual access, and so on.

By definition, the language that generates the expression is a solution to all these empirical conditions. Rational enquiry is the attempt to find the best theory that satisfies all the empirical conditions—that is just the nature of the game. If you are not playing that game, you are not doing science. So, by definition, the language is a solution to all the empirical conditions and we want to find the best theory we can of that solution.

But we are asking a different question here. We are looking only at a certain sub-part of the empirical conditions, namely the legibility conditions, the conditions of readability, of access to the expression by the outside systems. So, for example, the sensorimotor systems will require that the expression has a temporal order (sensorimotor systems are so constructed that they can only deal with something that goes through time; that is not logically necessary by any means). It is a fact about our sensorimotor systems that they require certain kinds of phonetic properties and rhythmic patterns, and so on. If an expression doesn't have those things, the sensorimotor apparatus won't be able to 'read' it, to perceive it, to articulate it. The conceptual-intentional systems, which we don't know much about, are plainly going to require certain kinds of information about words and phrases and certain kind of relations among them, and so on.[15] There are also, in addition to that, sound-meaning relations; but those are well beyond the legibility conditions. The fact that 'John had a book stolen' has a certain multiple ambiguity does not follow from the fact that at the interface levels, its elements can be accessed. So, whatever the sound-meaning relations are, they are something over and above the property of being accessible to the several performance systems, the property of having the right kind of phonetic and semantic representations, interface representations.

If human language is perfect in a very strong sense, then the sound-meaning relations, say, for the sentence I mentioned, or for any sentence in any language, will follow from an optimal solution to the legibility conditions, and the same will be true of the whole range of empirical properties of the expressions and of all expressions in all languages. The best theory that considers just satisfaction of the legibility conditions would remain the best theory when you add all the other conditions. You will not have to change it when you bring in other empirical conditions.

The study of language, for thousands of years, has assumed that you at least have to make use of sound-meaning relations to discover the properties of a language. All research assumes that. But this assumption is just what we are now questioning. We are entertaining the possibility that if we knew enough about the legibility conditions, the sound-meaning relations would follow. We wouldn't need them as evidence to determine the properties of particular languages and the same would be true of the whole vast array of other empirical evidence.

That is very strange. There's nothing in biology to suggest that anything like perfect design in this sense is a possibility. Nevertheless, there is some reason to suppose that language is surprisingly close to perfect in that very curious sense; that is, it is a near-optimal solution to the legibility conditions, or, what are sometimes called the 'bare output conditions'.[16] If that turns out to be even partially true, it is extremely surprising and, to that extent, extremely interesting.

It is also extremely interesting to try to identify and

investigate the apparent imperfections. The Minimalist Program is based on the assumption that this is a serious question as well. Then we have the following sort of intuitions to explore. One, we try to subject assumptions about language to very close scrutiny to see if they are empirically justified or are just a kind of technical convenience, obscuring gaps of understanding. Second, when there is any departure from perfection, from conceptual naturalness in satisfying just legibility conditions, we raise a question mark and ask if that departure is justified. In each case, when an assumption looks as though it is not conceptually necessary (given legibility conditions), what we do is to try to show that there is at least as good an account of the empirical facts if one doesn't make that assumption. More ambitiously, we might try to show that there is even a better account if we drop the assumption; that is, we get a deeper and a more far-reaching explanation with broader empirical scope if this extra technology is abandoned and we keep to the more perfect design. That is the programme.

Pursuing the programme, we face such problems as the following. First of all, you have to show that, contrary to what has always been believed, there are no linguistic levels apart from the interface levels themselves—the phonetic and the semantic representations. There shouldn't be any other levels because other levels are not motivated by legibility conditions. So, what you want to show is that they were just there as a technological device to cover up gaps of understanding. When you drop them you have better explanations; there's nothing like deep or surface structure in the technical sense, and everything that had been accounted for in terms of those levels was misunderstood and misdescribed. It is properly construed just in terms of interface levels. That is a pretty large task. Getting more technical, it means you've got to show that the projection principle is wrong,[17] that Binding and Case theory don't apply at S-structure as has always been assumed,[18] and so on for a host of other things.

The second problem that you have to deal with is to try to show that a lexical item, which is a collection of properties called 'features', contains no features other than those that are interpreted at the interface and that no elements are introduced along the way. So, no indices, no phrase structure per X-bar theory—all that has to go.[19] We have to show that when we abandon X-bar theory, indices, and other such devices, we find solutions which are not only as good but even better ones. That is the second major task.

The third major task is to show that there are no structural relations other than those that are forced by the legibility conditions (including such properties as adjacency, theta-structure, scope at LF) or, else, that are induced in some natural way by the process of derivation itself. Take, say, c-command.[20] C-command is the property that you have when you merge two structures and one of them is then related to pieces of the other; you know which one it is by output conditions because the one that is targeted is no longer visible, so it is the other one that c-commands (this is not going to mean anything to people who do not know what I am talking about). You can define c-command in those terms and, therefore, it is a legitimate relationship. Local relations to head are also legitimate relations but perhaps nothing else. That means there is no government, no proper government,[21] no Binding theory internal to language, and no interactions of other kinds. To the extent that language is perfect, all of this has got to go.

Those of you who are familiar with the technical literature (by now I am afraid I am narrowing the audience but I don't know how else to proceed) are aware that there is a ton of empirical evidence to support the opposite conclusion on every single point that I mentioned. Furthermore, the core assumption of the highly productive recent work—and its pretty impressive achievements—is that everything I just said is wrong; that is, languages are highly imperfect in all these respects, as indeed you would expect—they have indices and bar levels, D-structures, S-structures and all kinds of relations, and so on and so forth. So it is no small task to demonstrate the contrary. Nevertheless, I think the contrary could well be true.

Now there are what seem to be real imperfections and they are interesting ones. One dramatic imperfection in human language is the property of displacement which seems to be universal, looks rather intricate and is never built into symbolic systems that are designed for special uses which are sometimes called formal languages. What I mean by that is the pervasive fact that phrases are interpreted as if they were in some different position in the structure where such items sometimes are actually sounded. That is a property which is universal in language and it has enormous consequences for interpretations of sound and meaning. For example, take the sentence 'the book seems to have been stolen'. What is the relation between 'book' and 'steal'? You understand that to be the same relation as it is in 'John stole the book' where there is a natural, local relationship between 'steal' and 'book'[22] but there isn't that relationship in 'the book seems to have been stolen'. This displacement property is a general property of language.[23] It seems to be an imperfection—you don't build it into perfect systems that you are designing for special purposes but it is ubiquitous in natural language. The property has to be first of all explained and secondly captured somehow.

In early generative grammar, it was assumed that the property is captured by an operation that displaced the phrase from its position of interpretation to the position where it is pronounced. That operation is a grammatical transformation. Every theory of language has some way of capturing the displacement property; so they all have transformations or some counterpart.[24] The only question is what their form is because it is just a fact about language that it has this property. I think there is pretty good reason to believe that this original assumption is more or less correct. If so, then there is an operation of language that takes a structured phrase and attaches it somewhere else. The simplest assumption—the one you assume if you are minimally departing from perfection—would be that the operation is nothing more than that; you take a phrase that appeared somewhere and you attach it somewhere else. Notice that it would then follow that the phrase appears twice. It appears in the original position and in the place where you attached it, under the simplest assumptions.

The more complex assumption is that there is a compound operation—you take the phrase, you attach it somewhere else and then you delete the original—that is two operations, so it is more complex. On the surface, the more complex assumption looks correct—in fact you only hear it in one position. You don't hear 'the book seems to have been stolen [the book]' or, for those who know what I am talking about, you don't hear 'the book seems [the book] to have been stolen [the book]'. It is in three positions—that would actually have to be if you run through the process correctly. So it looks as if you have the more complex operation, not the simpler operation and that was in fact the original assumption. But it turns out to be wrong.

It turns out that there is very good evidence now that the phrase is in all those positions—in the original position, in the end position and in all the intermediate positions.[25] That fact has all sorts of consequences for semantic interpretation. So it means that whatever the mind is doing, it is seeing it in all those positions—that is the 'copy version' of trace theory. But it has almost always been mistakenly assumed that the 'copy theory' is more complex, that you have to justify it empirically.[26] The opposite is the case. The copy version of trace theory is the simplest assumption; it says that the only operation is the attachment operation. You have to justify the non-existence of this theory. It turns out that language is perfect enough so that the simplest assumption is correct, which has lots of consequences.

Why do you only hear the phrase once? This is because of a very superficial principle at the phonetic output interface that erases everything but one and it does it in a very general fashion.[27] But as far as the mind is concerned, they are all there; if you don't have to bother talking, they would all be there. In fact they are all there in the mental operations but just some of them are spelt out—one, in fact.

Why should language have this displacement property? That is an interesting question which has been discussed for about forty years without an awful lot of progress. But it does have the property and there are some ideas about why it should. These ideas can be reinterpreted in terms of legibility conditions at the surface. For example, there seems to be a fundamental difference between two kinds of semantic properties—'deep structure' and 'surface structure' properties in one conception, the latter relying on displacement of an item to a 'more prominent' position at the edge of a construction. If such ideas can be successfully developed, it might turn out that the displacement property is not an imperfection after all, but rather an externally-imposed legibility condition that human language must satisfy (but not special-purpose symbolic systems, which lack the 'surface semantics' of natural language, and do not have to satisfy the legibility conditions of natural language). Whatever the answer to the question about 'why',[28] it seems that this displacement principle is correct and that it is there universally; so, the problem is to determine its nature. That has been one of the central research topics for around forty years.

There is pretty good reason to believe that the core element of displacement, at the heart of the displacement property, is the fact that certain features of lexical items are not legible at the semantic interface, that they have no interpretation—they are there but have no interpretation. If they have no interpretation they have got to be erased; otherwise, the semantic interface is not going to be able to read the output. So there are features of lexical items which have to be erased by the computation somewhere if the expression is going to be legible. The only relations that exist are local relations, so they have to be brought into a local relationship with something that can erase them. But the element that can erase them often happens to be remote, so they have to be brought into a local relationship with it (and have to carry along bigger elements for independent reasons). That looks like the core of the displacement property, a technique for erasing features that are illegible at the output.

What kinds of features are these? One example is

structural case of nouns. So you understand, say, 'book', exactly the same way if it is in nominative case or accusative case or ergative or absolutive; it has exactly the same interpretation. So the property of structural case is not legible at the interface; it makes no difference to interpretation. So it has got to be eliminated. The only way to eliminate it is to take it and put it somewhere else in a local relation to something that can wipe it out. Then both will disappear and nothing is illegible. But that is going to yield the displacement property. The same is true of, say, agreement features of verbs. If a noun is singular or plural, you understand it differently. But if a verb is singular or plural, you understand it exactly the same way. So the agreement features of verbs are uninterpretable and they have got to be erased, which means something has to get into a local relation with them, and that is going to force movement of matching agreement features of nouns, and displacement of the phrase in which they appear. And so on across quite a range.

How local does the relation have to be? Possibly the relation is so local that it has to be internal to the word. That seems to be the case (that is not in Chapter four, incidentally; I'm beyond that now for those of you who know the book[29]). Uninterpretable features within a word have to be erased and that is the core of the displacement property. It turns out that quite a lot of things about language can be explained in those terms. So there seems to be an imperfection but a very narrow one having to do with non-interpretability of certain formal properties of lexical items, and it might be that this is no imperfection at all, but rather an optimal way of satisfying an externally-imposed legibility condition, if the speculation mentioned earlier proves to have some validity.

Apart from the displacement property which is, may be, reducible to feature movement and some automatic consequences, there is one other operation that in fact is necessary in a perfect system. It is necessary on purely conceptual grounds. That is an operation that takes two linguistic objects that have already been formed by the recursive procedures of generation, and constructs a larger one from them. So, if you have already formed 'the man' and 'stole the book', you can form 'the man stole the book'. Now on minimalist assumptions (that is, perfection assumptions), the generation of expressions should involve nothing more than these two operations—feature movement to erase illegible features, and merger—taking two constructions and putting them together. The full displacement operation combines these—attracting a matching feature to eliminate an uninterpretable feature, then merging a phrase containing the matching feature (if necessary for other reasons; sometimes it is not, and we have feature attraction alone, as in so-called 'long distance agreement').

That seems surprisingly close to the truth, once we discover the principles that govern the elementary operations—principles of locality, economy and so on, that radically constrain the way these operations are going to work. If that is correct, then the differences among languages are going to lie, to a very large measure, in the specific way in which the uninterpretable features (like, say, case and verbal agreement) are spelt out in different languages—with a whole range of consequences that you hope are going to follow automatically from the very narrow class of lexical properties, given the universal constraints.

Languages certainly look radically different in these respects. So, take Sanskrit which has a fairly rich system of overt inflections—you hear a lot of inflections. English has virtually none, Chinese has even less; so they look totally different. And, furthermore, they appear in structurally different positions all over the place in different languages, which means that you can't get anything remotely like word-by-word translations.

However, increasingly it is being found that these differences are superficial; that is, Chinese with no inflections and Sanskrit with a lot of inflections seem to be very similar, perhaps identical apart from peripheral lexical features. If so, then for the mind, they're the same. They differ only in the way in which the sensorimotor system accesses the uniform derivation. They all have the cases and agreement and everything else, even richer than Sanskrit; but only the mind sees them.

It seems also to be true of the positions in which words appear. They are basically all the same but the sensorimotor process accesses different aspects of the derivations that are formed in the mind. If such conclusions can be established over a broad range, we can pursue the basic quest of the Minimalist Program—to try to show that the universal properties themselves are explicable on principles of optimal design, given the requirement of legibility at the interface.

I have been talking about research directions, motivations. So far it has been pretty programmatic. To proceed further, we would have to carry out detailed empirical enquiry to evaluate these theoretical proposals. There is some material in print, more coming along the way.[30] How successful is it? Well, you have to judge. To me it looks pretty encouraging and pretty surprising, although how far these efforts can go is quite an open question and a pretty hard one. These are topics of a new order of difficulty in any of these domains, not often pursued in the special sciences generally.

If some version of this programme works out, we will have a picture of language that is surprising for a biological system. It is more similar in some ways to what you find in the study of the inorganic world where, for obscure reasons, attempts to show that things are perfectly designed often seem to work out. Nobody knows why. But it has been a very productive kind of intuition in the hard sciences to assume that things are really perfect. If you find numbers like seven, you have probably made a mistake; it has really got to be eight because eight is two cubed and two and three are proper numbers; but seven isn't, it is too complicated. That kind of intuition has been very productive in the hard sciences. These are kind of perfect-design assumptions but only for simple systems, discovered by far-reaching abstraction from the phenomenon of ordinary life. If something like that turns out to be true of language, it will be extremely surprising and very interesting.

My own feeling has always been that it is right in this area that the most interesting aspects of the study of language lie. It seems to have quite mysterious properties, unexpected properties, for biological systems, and the more closely we investigate it the more curious and mysterious it seems to be.

NOTES

[1] In his opening address, Rama Kant Agnihotri of Delhi University raised, among other things, the following questions: Why doesn't Chomsky's politics force him to look at language as an additional tool of exploitation in society? How does a person so deeply touched by human suffering reconcile with considering language as a purely biological cognitive system rather than an essential component of the sociological power-games?

² In Chomsky (1986a) these were labelled 'Plato's Problem' and 'Orwell's Problem', respectively. See Chomsky (1993b) for a discussion of possible relationships between these problems. See the references in Barsky (1997) for Chomsky's social and political views. See also Rai (1995) and the film mentioned in note 4 of the editor's preface. Since the present lecture does not explicitly concern Orwell's Problem, we did not include references to Chomsky's massive work in this area.

³ For some similarities and dissimilarities between the human visual system and the language faculty, see Chomsky (1980, chapter 6; 1988, chapter 5), among others.

⁴ The argument from poverty of stimulus. See Piattelli-Palmarini (1980) for extensive discussion. See Chomsky (1986a, chapter 1). See also Wexler (1991) for a discussion of the centrality of the argument in Chomsky's work.

⁵ See the discussion of I- and E-languages in Chomsky (1986a); also Chomsky (1991).

⁶ The following is a more detailed statement of the notion 'generate' in generative grammar, where 'structural descriptions' are essentially what Chomsky calls 'expressions' in the lecture:

> . . . (T)he grammar generates the sentences it describes and their structural descriptions; the grammar is said to 'weakly generate' the sentences of a language and to 'strongly generate' the structural descriptions of these sentences. When we speak of the linguist's grammar as a 'generative grammar', we mean only that it is sufficiently explicit to determine how sentences in the language are in fact characterized by the grammar. (Chomsky 1980: 220)

⁷ See Chomsky (1993a, 1994, 1995c) for recent discussions of these topics.

⁸ The following are among the many syntactic phenomena ignored by such grammars:

(a) Constructions that are understood as having more than one interpretation: 'Flying planes can be dangerous', 'I had a book stolen', etc.

(b) Constructions that appear to have the same structure, but indeed do not, since they are understood differently.

     (i) I persuaded John to leave/I expected John to leave.

    (ii) the growling of the lions/the raising of flowers/the shooting of the hunters (ambiguous).

   (iii) John is easy to please/John is eager to please.

(c) Sentences that bear paraphrase relationship with each other, but do not have the same structure:

I expected a specialist to examine John.

I expected John to be examined by a specialist.

(d) The difference in the grammatical status of sentences such as the following (an instance of what came to be known as 'subject–object asymmetry'):

*Who does he think that Mary saw?

Who does he think Mary saw?

*Who does he think that came?

Who does he think came?

(e) Interpretation of understood elements in constructions such as:

John persuaded Mary to go.

John promised Mary to go.

The police stopped drinking.

See Chomsky (1957, 1965) among others. As far as complex and quite interesting properties of lexical items ignored by standard dictionaries are concerned, see Chomsky (1988, 1993a, 1996).

[9] See Chomsky (1965, chapter 1), for a classic discussion of descriptive and explanatory adequacies.

[10] See Chomsky et al. (1982).

[11] See Chomsky (1991) for a succinct statement of this point.

[12] Chomsky often uses a very lucid metaphor to express the same idea:

We can think of the initial state of the faculty of language as a fixed network connected to a switchbox; the network is constituted of the principles of language, while the switches are the options to be determined by experience. When the switches are set in one way, we have Bantu; when they are set another way, we have Japanese. Each particular human language is identified as a particular setting of switches ... (Chomsky 1997, Part 1, p. 6).

[13] See the informal discussion in Chomsky et al. (1982) on the significance of the principles and parameters framework; also, chapter 1 of Chomsky (1995b) for a more recent exposition.

[14] The sentence is ambiguous in the following ways: (a) someone stole John's book, (b) John had someone steal a book, and (c) John had almost succeeded in stealing a book. See Chomsky (1965: 22).

[15] The conceptual-intentional systems access/read the level of linguistic representation called 'Logical Form' (LF), where such information is said to be available. See Chomsky (1991) where he lists the following elements that LF representations must contain:

1. Arguments, which are A-chains headed by and terminating with an element in A-position, the latter theta-marked, the former case-marked

2. Adjuncts, which are A-bar chains, headed and terminated by elements in A-bar positions

3. Lexical elements, which are chains headed and terminated by elements in X^0-positions

4. Predicates, possibly predicate chains if there is predicate raising, VP-movement in syntax and so on

5. Operator-variable constructions, each a two-membered chain (X_1, X_2), where the operator, X_1, is in an A-bar position and the variable, X_2, is in an A-position.

These are the legitimate LF objects. Similarly there are legitimate PF objects. The principle FI (Full Interpretation) ensures that only legitimate objects occur at interface levels, PF and LF.

See also Chomsky (1995b, chapter 2).

[16] For instance, the requirement that a constituent in a sentence be thematized (i.e. receive focus): 'fish' as in 'fish I like'. In terms of the 'VP-internal subject' hypothesis (see note 29 of Discussion below), both 'fish' and 'I' originate within the VP, and both are extracted out of the VP. 'Fish' is extracted so that it is topicalized (receive focus). Extraction of 'I' need not concern us here.

[17] The Projection Principle, as stated in Chomsky (1981), is as

follows:

Representations at each syntactic level (i.e. LF, and D- and S- structure) are projected from the lexicon, in that they observe the subcategorization properties of lexical items.

To give some examples of subcategorization properties of lexical items, the verb 'hit' must take a noun phrase (NP) as direct object, 'die' must not take any object, 'give' must take an NP and a prepositional phrase (PP).

The principle was augmented with the additional requirement that a clause must have a subject, and in its modified form was called 'Extended Projection Principle' (EPP). See Chomsky (1982). Subsequently, this additional requirement alone came to be known as EPP. Now in the Minimalist conception of grammar, which dispenses with D- and S-structure representations, and does not disallow LF representations that yield gibberish, there is no place for the original projection principle (Chomsky 1995b, chapter 3). As far as the augmented requirement (EPP) is concerned, it is now captured in a different way: the head (I) of the Inflectional Phrase (IP) has the 'strong' feature that it must have a subject. See Chomsky (1995b: 232) for more technical details.

[18] Binding theory is concerned with assignment of antecedents to anaphors ('himself', 'each other', etc.), specifying which NPs in a sentence cannot be antecedents of pronouns ('he', 'them', etc.) and ensuring that r-expressions ('John', 'The nice weather', etc.) remain antecedent-free in a clause.

Case theory (the theory of Abstract Case) has essentially two aspects:

(a) Assignment of (abstract) case to lexical NPs, that is, those with phonetic content; however see Chomsky (1986a), where it is suggested that 'PRO', lacking such content, has Case. 'PRO' ('pronominal anaphor') is the so-called 'understood subject' in infinitival constructions, as in 'John wants [[PRO] to go home]', where the outer bracketing indicates the infinitival clause.

(b) Evaluation of a string as ungrammatical that contains a lexical NP without Case (called 'Case filter').

These were supposed to apply at the level of S-structure, but in the more recent Minimalist Program that dispenses with S-structure, Case checking and assignment of antecedents to anaphors etc. take place elsewhere. The tasks of the Binding theory have to be performed at the LF level. Case assignment is no longer required since NPs enter the derivation already inflected with Case features; Case filter can now be viewed as an interface condition which requires that Case checking be done during the derivation itself. See Chomsky (1995b: chapter 3) for details.

[19] Subscripting, superscripting and coindexing play a crucial role in the so-called government-Binding (GB) theory. Binding (anaphor-antecedent etc.) relations are expressed in terms of cosubscripting, and non-binding ones (such as between 'it' and the extraposed clause: 'it is true that John is honest') and subject-AGR in terms of cosuperscripting. Indices attach to entities during derivation. See Chomsky (1981) for details.

A 'phrase' has been viewed as a basic syntactic object. According to GB theory, all of the following from traditional grammar are instances of phrases: main, coordinate and subordinate clauses, phrases and single words ('John', 'he'). In addition, 'PRO', the understood nominal element, is also an instance of a phrase. In earlier versions of modern generative grammar, phrase-structure rules (PS rules) captured the internal structure of phrases. Some versions of generative grammar, such as Lexical Functional Grammar (LFG), still do so. Attempts have been made to eliminate PS rules altogether, and whatever remains of them in the GB model is in the form of X-bar schemata.

X-bar theory was proposed in the late sixties. One important thing it did was to capture the common internal structure of all phrases (X″) in terms of head (X), specifier and complement. In this scheme, a phrase is viewed as the maximal projection of its head: for example, the noun phrase (NP) ('the destruction of the city') is the maximal projection of the noun (N) ('destruction'); the verb phrase (VP) ('destroyed the city') is the maximal projection of the verb

(V) ('destroy'), and so on. Head-initial languages (e.g. English) have the head-complement order, and head-final ones (e.g. Hindi) have complement-head order. The internal structure of any phrase in head-initial languages is:

$[_{x''}\text{SPEC } [_{x''}[_x\text{HEAD] COMPLEMENT}]]$

The X-bar organization can be viewed as a template given by UG. It is a constraint that PS rules have to meet in a grammar which has such rules. See Chomsky (1972b) for details. See also Chomsky (1995a) for an execution of the idea that X-bar theory can be dispensed with.

[20] C-command is a structural relation between two entities in a hierarchical configuration. There are more than one definitions of this relation in the literature. One definition is as follows:

An entity A c-commands an entity B iff every maximal projection that dominates A dominates B.

In the following configuration, V c-commands NP and PP

$[_{v''}[_{v'} \text{ V NP] PP}]$

In terms of yet another definition of c-command, V c-commands NP, but not PP.

[21] Government and proper government are structural relations between two entities in a tree configuration. The former is essentially a locality notion, required for a range of cases: binding, Case etc. The latter is a requirement that traces of moved constituents must satisfy.

Definitions:

Government: A governs B iff (a) A c-commands B (b) A is a head, and (c) every maximal projection that dominates B dominates A.

Proper Government: A properly governs B iff (a) A governs B and A is lexical, or (b) A locally A-bar binds B.

For details, see Chomsky (1981, 1986b), and Lasnik and Saito (1984), among others. In the Minimalist Program, these notions are no longer needed. More basic locality relations, such as specifier-head, head-complement etc., render the notion of government superfluous. For example, the notion of a governor need not be involved in Case-

and Theta theories; their effects are captured in terms of the above relations. As far as proper government is concerned, it essentially reduces to economy conditions of various types. See Chomsky (1995b), especially chapters 3 and 4, for technical details.

[22] The relationship between 'steal' and 'book' is the familiar verb–object relationship (one instance of 'head-complement' relationship in X-bar theoretic terms), which is very local, and is in some sense semantic. In contrast, there is no semantic relationship between 'seem' and 'book' (compare the relationship between 'John' and 'sleep' in 'John slept', which is semantic); besides, 'book' occurs in a different clause (that is, the main clause) from the one in which it receives its semantic interpretation (the subordinate clause).

[23] For more technical and conceptual details regarding the property of displacement as an imperfection in language, see Chomsky (1995b: 4.7.1; 1997).

[24] Lexical Functional Grammar (LFG), for example, claims to be a (generative but) non-transformational grammar. It has PS rules, but no transformational rules in the familiar sense. However, Chomsky's point is that the technical devices that such non-transformational grammars as LFG and Generalized Phrase Structure Grammars (GPSG) use, in place of transformational rules to account for displacement facts, are nothing but mere equivalents of transformational rules. For details regarding LFG, see Bresnan (1982); for GPSG, see Gazdar et al. (1985).

[25] This illustrates the so-called copy theory of movement. Informally speaking and ignoring many details, when move-∝ displaces a constituent, a copy of the same is left at the original place. The constituent is pronounced at the target site and is assigned semantic (more technically, thematic) interpretation at the place of its origin. The moved constituent and its copy constitute a chain.

The question is whether there is any justification for the copy at the *intermediate* place, where it is neither pronounced nor interpreted. There indeed is some justification which comes from structures such as the following:

* 'John seems it to have been expected to leave'. The impossibility of having 'it' in the subject position of the subordinate clause shows that the place is already filled with the copy of the moved constituent 'John'; in other words, 'John' has not leapt from the subject position of the infinitive clause directly to the subject position of the main clause, but it has reached there 'successive cyclically'. For details, see Chomsky (1995b).

26 See Chomsky (1975) for an informal account of trace-theory.

27 For some discussion, see Chomsky (1995b, especially chapters 1 and 3).

28 See Fodor (1987), Jackendoff (1990).

29 The reference is to Chomsky (1995b)

30 Some of this literature is available in the recent issues of *Linguistic Inquiry, Linguistics and Philosophy*, and other journals. For book-length work, see the recent items (such as Kitahara 1997, Brody 1995, Zubizarreta 1998, Barbosa *et al.* 1998 etc.) in the Linguistic Inquiry Monograph Series of the MIT Press.

Discussion

The audience was invited to ask questions and submit these also in writing to save time. Rama Kant Agnihotri of Delhi University chaired the session. The following conversation ensued.

Chomsky (to Agnihotri): Why don't I read them myself; that'll make it simpler.

Agnihotri: I was trying to classify them but it seems . . .

Chomsky: Okay, you want to do that; let's do that.

Agnihotri: If you could treat these questions first; I'll keep giving you more.

Chomsky: That is censorship, some censorship is going on here.

SCOPE OF LINGUISTICS

QUESTION: With the growth of a 'Chomskyan era', linguistics has definitely become a discipline worth breaking heads over. At the same time it has become so esoteric that it has become restricted to people holding a job in linguistics only. How do you think this subject can become accessible to people beyond linguistics? What about its marketability?

CHOMSKY: I don't like this personalization. That is a wrong way to think about things. There is no personalization in rational enquiry, everybody is working on it. But I'll leave the question the way it sounds.

Well, first of all, a lot of linguistics is accessible. You could ask the same question about chemistry. An awful lot of chemistry is just unintelligible unless you have been through a pretty extensive education to know what people are talking about, understand the results, the background, the principles, and so on. But basic ideas can be made accessible to people quite readily. That is what popular science is about. Making the results of a technical enquiry accessible to people, at whatever level they want to understand it, is a very legitimate and socially valuable occupation. So if I am interested in learning something about quantum physics, I don't want to bother with all the details; I just want to understand roughly what is going on. There are people and books and so on that try to make it available at my level of interest. I think the same is true in linguistics.[1]

What about marketability? Jobs are certainly a problem. When you get into any field that gets hard and complicated, there's always a question about where you are going to get a job. That is just as true in mathematics as it is in linguistics. Right now in the United States, there are, on an average, several hundred applicants for every available professional position in mathematics. That is a problem. It is not just a problem for linguistics; in fact it is, in many ways, less of a problem for linguistics.

In any case, it is a general problem. It does have to do

with a social problem—how much science should there be? Right now the answer to that question is given, in my view, extremely irrationally. It is not a big secret that wealth and power are very highly concentrated and the people in whose hands it is concentrated make the decisions. The way they make the decisions is largely by deciding what they want from the point of view of market value. That is an extremely irrational way for social decisions to be made. These decisions, like all decisions, should be popular decisions made on the basis of judgements as to where resources ought to go.

In my opinion, there ought to be a lot more science and everybody ought to be involved in it in some sense just like there ought to be a lot more literature and art. These are the enriching parts of human life; they should be made accessible to people. That means we should devote resources to them. But you don't make money for businesses that way and, since that is how jobs and resources are distributed, you get the results you have. I think that is pretty irrational but that has to do with lack of democracy in society in general.

QUESTION: What is in common between your science of language and your politics is the absence of any role of community and culture. The conscience of the community is what finds expression in justice as well as in language. In the study of language, don't you think better results will be obtained from giving positive values to the differences between languages, to relations of complementarity between two or more languages spoken simultaneously by the same community and by supposing the state of bilingualism to be normal to the species?

CHOMSKY: My political views are my own. Anything that one says about politics, of course, has to do with community and culture. How could it be otherwise? That is true not only of attempts to understand the world, but also to change it. In my own personal case, the point should be particularly obvious, if only because of my interest in and commitment to anarchism—specifically, those tendencies within it that stressed the significance of community, association and culture.

The science of language is not mine. It is anybody's who is working on it; people don't own a science. So it is not Chomsky's science of language. The search for understanding of how the world works is a co-operative enterprise, and nothing that could be called 'X's science of Y' is even worth looking at. There's a field that is often called 'generative grammar', but it is not mine, or anyone else's.

This branch of the study of language is indeed marked by an absence of any role for community and culture, but that is for the reason I mentioned earlier. There is nothing of any significance known, at least to me, about community and culture that relates to these questions about the nature of a certain biological system. If there is something known, I'll be glad to learn about it but I don't know about it. Therefore, as far as I am aware, there is no relationship.

But that is not to say that questions about community, culture and language are unimportant. They are extremely important but so is everything about human life; it is just that we have little scientific understanding of them. We ought to be very clear and explicit about what we understand, what we have technical knowledge of, and when we are in the same boat as everybody else. We just try to find our way through it as well as we can but without theoretical understanding of any depth. If that is wrong, I am happy to be instructed, but I don't know of any reason to believe that it is wrong.

Everyone working on language, myself included, focuses attention on 'differences between languages'. If we didn't, we would conclude that whatever language we happen to be looking at is innate—which would certainly 'solve' a lot of questions about the language faculty, language acquisition, etc. The first modern work on generative grammar happened to be on Hebrew.[2] The first generative grammar published was on Hidatsa.[3] So it continues. It is not a matter of 'better results' or 'worse results', any more than one could answer the question whether we get 'better results' or 'worse results' by studying just hydrogen or the differences between hydrogen and helium, or just fruit flies and not the difference between fruit flies and apes. At any moment, one concentrates on questions that look promising.

As to the positive value of differences between languages and bilingualism and so on, I really don't have any considered opinion on this. Obviously, you're a richer person if you have more diverse kinds of experience; that is certainly true. So exposure to various cultures and immersion in various cultures, languages and so on adds a certain richness to life and, yes, richness to life has a positive value; but I don't know what more there is to say about this.

Bilingualism is normal to the species in the trivial sense that the world is so complex that strict monolingualism is almost unimaginable. Even in the smallest, hunter-gatherer society with fifteen people in the tribe, there's going to be diversity. People aren't clones and as long as there is some diversity, you're going to have some small variety of multilingualism. It may be so small that you won't call it 'multilingualism' but there will be some variety. In that sense it is natural to the species but I don't see anything deep about that.

It is also well to bear in mind that 'multilingualism' is a vague intuitive notion; every person is multiply multi-lingual in a more technical sense. To say that people speak different languages is a bit like saying they live in differ-ent places or look different, notions that are perfectly useful for ordinary life, but are highly interest-relative. We say that a person speaks several languages, rather than several varieties of one, if the differences matter for some purpose or interest.

QUESTION: Do you treat music as a language?

CHOMSKY: I don't have anything special to say on this but there are people who have worked on it. The best study I know is by Ray Jackendoff and Fred Lerdahl.[4] Lerdahl is a professional composer and Jackendoff is a professional linguist and also, virtually, a professional musician. The two of them did a book on the linguistic aspects of music which is quite interesting. They studied a narrow range of music (classical western music with tonal centres) and tried to show that it has quasi-linguistic pro-perties. You can read the book and find out how convinced you are. The book was actually written as a kind of response to an effort by Leonard Bernstein to do something similar.[5]

Now suppose that they are right; does it follow that music is a language? That is not a meaningful question be-cause the notion of what is a language is not a meaningful notion. Is it a human language? No, of course not; it is not a human language. Is it *like* human language? Well, sure, in some ways but then the question is: how 'like' do you mean?

To say that something is a language is not a meaningful comment; it is just to say—'it is enough like human language so that I'll call it "language".' It is like asking: does somebody live near Boston? There is no definite answer to that. If I am talking to a friend at home and we were talking about how to get to work in Boston, I could ask him, 'do you live near Boston?'; if he lives ten miles away, farther away than I do, he would say 'no'. If, on the other hand, I am talking to you here in Delhi and I ask, 'does he live near Boston?', the answer would be 'yes' because, from a different perspective, he lives near Boston. Similarly, there is no meaningful question, 'is something a language?' We can ask whether it is like human language in some respects. And if we happen to feel interested in those resemblances, we may decide to call it 'a language'. It is a terminological question.

QUESTION: Don't you think that DNA coding of viruses is a language?

CHOMSKY: The question can't be answered because the notion of 'language' is too imprecise. It is a bit like asking whether airplanes 'really fly' (like eagles) but submarines don't 'really swim' (like dolphins) and people don't 'really fly' when they jump over a bar in the Olympic games. In English, we speak of airplanes (but not people) flying but not of submarines swimming. Usage is different in other languages.[6] These are not factual questions; rather, questions about whether to adopt certain metaphorical usages. Same with DNA coding and language.

There could well be interesting general questions about what airplanes, people and eagles do when they spend time off the ground, maybe something about principles of aerodynamics. And there could well be interesting questions about the relation of DNA coding and the specific biological system, human language (some serious scientists have been asking them). How interesting? That we will know after the results are in, not before.

QUESTION: It is known that the deaf have inner speech. Is this based on semantics or syntax?

CHOMSKY: People lacking exposure to spoken language may or may not have something that resembles what we call 'inner speech'. We certainly are conscious of what seems very much like use of language but without articulation, though sensorimotor systems could be involved; and perhaps something like that is true of humans generally. As for whether these systems have 'syntax' or 'semantics', we have to clarify first what we mean by these terms. If we mean them in the sense of most of the modern 'theory of signs', then they surely have syntax (that is, modes of organization of the symbolic elements of which they are constituents), but may or may not have 'semantics' (that is, a purported relation between symbols and things of the non-mental world to which they 'refer'). There are non-trivial questions lurking here, for ordinary spoken language as well.[7]

QUESTION: Sign language or verbal language—which is a better option in the context of deficits in the sensorimotor interface as far as hearing-impaired children are concerned?

CHOMSKY: It depends on the circumstances. If my neighbours had a hearing-impaired child and asked my advice, I would say, first, that I'm not particularly qualified to give advice about what is best for their child; and second, that the advice of people with real training and experience should be heeded and evaluated, but with the recognition that even they have only very limited understanding of such intricate matters. And then, if my advice is still wanted, I'd suggest that the child be introduced to both sign language and spoken language, in as natural a setting as possible.

QUESTION: Is there a connection between language and sexuality as Jacques Laćan has posited in his theory of subjectivity?

CHOMSKY: I knew Laćan personally and I never understood a word he was talking about; so I can't answer the question. In fact I have a rather strong feeling that he was playing jokes, that he was trying to see how crazy he could be and still get people to take him seriously. I can't prove it to be true but that is my suspicion. We got along fine, we talked about all sorts of topics, but we never talked about these things.[8]

QUESTION: Do you consider semiotics as a science as we do for linguistics of today?

CHOMSKY: Semiotics is whatever it is. As much understanding of it as you have, that is what you have. To me it doesn't look very profound. I was once in an international conference together with Dan Sperber, a French semiotician and who is one of the leading specialists in the field. He was supposed to give a talk on semiotics. He got up, went to the blackboard and drew a big circle; he wrote in it 'language'. Then next to it he put in a little circle and he drew an arrow pointing to it which said 'traffic lights'. Then he turned towards the audience and said, 'That is semiotics'. He was exaggerating of course but there is something sort of true about the point he was trying to make. A lot is known about one of those things, language; there's not much to say about traffic lights. There are other big topics like cinema, art, human relations, and those are terribly important topics but I don't think you learn much about them from semiotics. You have to decide that for yourselves.

QUESTION: It is said that *homo sapiens* has the advantage of the faculty of language. Is it possible that actually the animals are better off than us because their system of communication is very sophisticated (saying more with less)?

CHOMSKY: I don't see any serious way to pose the question of who is 'better off'—ants, birds, humans, whatever. There are no standards of comparison. Keeping just to communication systems, one finds all sorts in the organic world, including humans (gesture systems, etc.). Human language is used for communication too, as is virtually everything that people do, but here too, comparisons seem useless. Some animal communication systems could be regarded as in some (not very meaningful) sense even 'richer' than natural language—continuous, as contrasted with the discrete infinity of human language, an unusual property of organisms.[9]

During the lively eighteenth-century debates on whether apes have language, one proposal was that they do, but are smart enough to realize that if they manifested this capacity, humans would put them to work as slaves; so they prefer to keep quiet when people are around. I always liked that one.

QUESTION: You said that it is in the overall architectural design of the human brain that the language acquisition device has a particular place with some kind of an interface but this interface is lacking in the case of primates. Do you mean to say that even animals have a language device but since they don't possess an appropriate interface capability they are not able to use a language?

CHOMSKY: I did say that but as a kind of joke. I said it is a possibility (it is a theoretical possibility); there is nothing we know about the natural world that tells us that it is false that apes actually have a language faculty but have no access to it. That is possible but there is no reason to believe it. So, yes, there is a possibility and, maybe, some day we will discover it to be true but nobody expects it; it is more likely that they don't have a language faculty.

Either way it is kind of hard to explain. There is no known explanation for most of the complex properties of organisms. People talk about Darwinian evolution and that sort of thing, but that doesn't really give you the answers beyond simple questions. Not just in the case of things like language. Take biological organisms like viruses—very simple organisms. They have certain structural properties like polyhedral shells. To attribute that to 'natural selection' would be missing the point.

Or, take the mathematical series called the 'Fibonacci series'. It shows up all over the place in nature; nobody knows exactly why. If you take a sunflower and you look at the flower, it has spirals that go in different directions.

The number of parts that appear in adjacent spirals are related to one another as successive terms in the Fibonacci series. You find that kind of thing all over nature; it is not well understood why. There is something about the physical world that forces certain kinds of structures to emerge under particular conditions.[10] If you can't explain what a sunflower looks like, you are not likely to be able to explain what natural language looks like; it is way more complicated. So, the fact that we do not know how to give serious evolutionary explanation of this is not surprising; that is not often possible beyond simple cases.

ACQUISITION OF LANGUAGE

QUESTION: Would you please elaborate your views upon the statement that language is innate but it also has an overlaid function both at the articulatory and the representational levels?

CHOMSKY: Well, the issue of innateness of language is a curious one. There is a huge literature arguing against the innateness of language; there's nothing defending the thesis. So the debate is kind of funny in that it is one-sided. Lots of people reject the proposal that language is innate but nobody ever answers them. The reason why nobody answers is that the arguments make no sense. There's no way to answer them.

To say that 'language is not innate' is to say that there is no difference between my granddaughter, a rock and a rabbit. In other words, if you take a rock, a rabbit and my granddaughter and put them in a community where people are talking English, they'll all learn English. If people believe that, then they believe that language is not innate.

If they believe that there is a difference between my granddaughter, a rabbit and a rock, then they believe that language is innate. So people who are proposing that there is something debatable about the assumption that language is innate are just confused. So deeply confused that there is no way of answering their arguments. There is no doubt that language is an innate faculty.

To say 'language is innate' is to express the belief that some crucial and relevant internal nature differentiates my granddaughter from rocks, bees, cats and chimpanzees. We want to find out what this internal nature is. On current understanding, it is an expression of genes, which somehow yields a language faculty (and, for example, a well-placed bone of the inner ear—in this case for mice as well). How is unknown, but that is true for vastly simpler questions as well. The informal statement that language is innate to humans means something like this. Similarly, we say that arms are innate to humans and wings to birds.

Now a question that could be asked is whether whatever is innate about language is specific to the language faculty or whether it is just some combination of the other aspects of the mind. That is an empirical question and there is no reason to be dogmatic about it; you look and you see. What we seem to find is that it is specific. There are properties of the language faculty, which are not found elsewhere, not only in the human mind, but in other biological organisms as far as we know.

For example, the most elementary property of the language faculty is the property of discrete infinity; you have six-word sentences, seven-word sentences but you don't have six-and-a-half-word sentences. Furthermore, there is no limit; you can have ten-word sentences, twenty-word sentences and so on indefinitely. That is the property of discrete infinity. This property is virtually unknown in the biological world. There are plenty of continuous systems, plenty of finite systems but try to find a system of discrete infinity! The only other one that anybody knows is the arithmetical capacity, which could well be some offshoot of the language faculty.[11] The more you go on the more it seems true.[12]

When you get to questions of the kind we've been discussing here, there seems to be no analogue elsewhere in the biological world down to the level of, maybe, DNA or some level where you are talking about biochemistry really. So it looks as though language is not only innate but highly specific in rather crucial respects. I take it that that is what is meant by the question of 'overlay'. It is an overlay to other things, it is something inserted into a system that has other properties. That is where empirical enquiry leads you. If somebody can think of some other explanation of the facts, it'll be interesting to hear it. But there's no other proposal, so there's nothing to discuss.

The problem is to discover to what extent properties of language and its use are specific to this system. Thus, we may ask whether the tongue and teeth are specifically adapted for language use in some way, or did they evolve independently of language. Opinions vary, though on some matters (say, the migration of the reptilian jawbone to the inner ear), the answers seem pretty clear. Some of the most respected scientists studying speech analysis and perception doubt that there are any specific adaptations of sensorimotor systems to language; others disagree.[13]

As for the far harder problem of representational levels, there are also varying opinions and interesting ideas, but naturally far less is understood. Suppose, for example, that one believes that an expression of natural language is mapped to the 'language of thought' (LOT).[14] Some properties of the expression must determine to which expression of LOT the linguistic expression is mapped. Which aspects of the interpretation of the expression are part of the language faculty, and which belong to the 'semantics of LOT'? There are speculations, but not much more.

QUESTION: Talking about 'analogies' for explanations,[15] is the notion of an 'organ' for language descriptive or analogical? I am not knowledgeable, but I am thinking of biogeneticians talking of a 'mobile brain' as opposed to the view of the brain as a commanding (central) organ. As a sociologist, I am working away from the notion of centre (equals to authority). Does it mean anything from your viewpoint?

CHOMSKY: The empirical question is whether there is a component of the brain (and possibly other systems of the body) which is specifically dedicated to language. If so, we can reasonably call that sub-system an 'organ', as in standard (though imprecise) usage, even in technical literature.[16] Nothing very profound is at stake. There is also no reason to introduce connotations about authority, any more than if we discover that parts of the cortex control the motion of my fingers as I type. The structure of organisms is what it is, and we try to come to understand it as best we can.

QUESTION: What about Broca's type of mapping, which is really not accurate, and the implications that this has for the 'location' of the language faculty?

CHOMSKY: However uncertain and variable it may be,

Broca's area is well defined enough to have been studied productively for many years, and is generally assumed to be one of the parts of the brain involved in language use. The non-intrusive technologies that are now becoming available are likely to yield better understanding of the ways in which the brain is implicated in knowledge and the use of language (the 'language organ' and its functioning). For the present, these questions remain elusive.[17] We should also bear in mind that in the informal sense in which the term 'organ' is used in biology, one does not necessarily expect to find a 'location'; the term is intended to focus attention on what appear to be components of complex systems, with identifiable properties and functions. A technical discussion that refers to the circulatory system or immune system as 'organs' does not mean to imply that they can be cut out of the body, leaving the rest intact.

QUESTION: What is the difference between LAD, the language acquisition device, and Universal Grammar?

CHOMSKY: None. They are just two different ways of looking at the same thing. Universal Grammar is the name for the theory of the initial state of the language faculty. LAD is another name for the initial state, just looking at it from a different point of view. So there's no difference.

QUESTION: What is the nature of the language acquisition device?

CHOMSKY: Well, whatever the nature of language is, that is what it is. According to one model, presumably oversimplified, if we understand the principles and the parameters of language, we will know what the language acquisition device is. It is something which has those principles and which has to fix those parameters and, when they are fixed, you get a language. In general, the 'language acquisition device' is whatever mediates between the initial state of the language faculty and the states that it can attain, which is another way of saying it is a description of the initial state.

QUESTION: Is there a contradiction in the claim that language is genetically determined and that it is like the visual system which requires external stimulation?

CHOMSKY: No, there's no contradiction in that. Let's take the visual system. This wasn't known forty years ago, but now it is known that the visual system of mammals, including us, has a highly intricate form that is genetically determined. But unless an appropriate kind of stimulation is given to it at a certain early period in infancy (pattern-stimulation, basically), then the system will deteriorate. It won't function. So it needs stimulation in order to function. Furthermore the kind of stimulation it gets will modify slightly the ways in which it functions.

Here's the basic experiment.[18] Cats have a visual system close enough to ours; so the results are probably more or less the same. If you take a cat, a kitten, and you sew its eyes closed (so it doesn't get any stimulation) and you stick electrodes in the striate cortex, you can see the degeneration of the biologically-determined structures after a couple of weeks. If you take a cat and you put something like half of a ping-pong ball over its eyes (so it gets diffused light but no patterns), you get the same result. If on the other hand you give it changing patterns of stimulation, the system functions. If you give it pattern-stimulation which consists solely of vertical lines, it will have a different distribution of cells in the striate cortex than if you give it pattern-stimulation that has horizontal lines. So it is a kind of a different language, if you like. It'll have a different state depending on the kind of pattern-stimulation it has. So there is no doubt that, in the mammalian visual system (there you can experiment), certain kinds of stimulation at particular points of life are necessary for the system to function at all and there is some variation in the way it functions depending on the kind of stimulation.

As far as we know, language is sort of like that. For ethical reasons, you can't do similar experiments in this case; so we don't know for sure that it is. You don't do experiments with infants this way unless you had, say, Joseph Mengele around. He would be happy to do experiments with infants which might give us the answers to these questions. Fortunately, you don't, although I should say that it is not that far back in the history of medicine where that was considered normal (ugly stories that are kept under the rugs in medical schools). But the fact is you nowadays don't do those kind of experiments. So we don't know the answers for sure but it is probably about the same. You need certain kinds of stimulation to get the system functioning and the forms of that stimulation apparently modify some of the ways in which it functions; Hindi versus English, let's say. It looks kind of like that.

There's a very interesting question as to whether children, raised in isolation (so that they never heard language at all) develop language. [Intervention from the audience] Pardon? Well, the wolf-children is not a very good example. There are some natural cases of children who have been brought up in isolation. The trouble is that they are so psychotic and there is so much wrong with them that you just don't know what to say about language.

The best-studied case is that of a girl who is given the name of 'Genie'; there's a book about her.[19] She was found, when she was about twelve or thirteen, locked in an attic. She had an insane father who had locked her up when she was about two years old, I think. She was tied to a chair and he sort of threw food at her now and then; so she was kept alive. But she apparently never heard any language after the age of two, except maybe something coming in from the window. A social worker found her and took her out. She was put in a hospital and people tried to help her.

There was also a study done on what she was able to do and there are some interesting results. But the trouble is you really don't quite know what they mean because she was psychotic, not surprisingly. There was so much psychic disorder that you don't know what part was language deficit. She never was able to get to anything like grammar. She could sort of communicate, she learned words, but she never learned anything like grammatical structure. But you really don't know what this means because there is too much disorder. It is like taking a computer and hitting it with a hammer and smashing it up and then trying to figure out how a computer works. It is not the way to do experiments.

On the other hand, there is one case of a natural experiment which sheds some light on this question. It involved three deaf children who were cousins or something; so they played together a lot. Their parents had been drilled with an unfortunate idea (that used to be conventional, isn't so much anymore) that sign language is bad for deaf children, that they have to learn lip-reading. Their parents had been indoctrinated with this belief to the extent that they were told not even to gesture to the children. So don't make hand-gestures because that'll get them to learn sign language. And apparently the parents kept to this pretty rigidly. So the children didn't hear anything because they were deaf and they didn't see anything much in the way of gestures or sign language.

Nevertheless, it was found that the three of them had invented their own sign language. The parents didn't know it because the children just used it among themselves. When it was discovered, a couple of very good psychologists—Lila Gleitman and her students—began to look at it carefully.[20] It turned out that the system that they had invented was a very interesting one. It was very much like ordinary human language; it was kind of an ergative-absolutive language[21] and they had about the level of development and complexity of children in normal environments. So it looked like they were developing a normal human language through their own modality, of course. The experiment ended at that point because as soon as they were discovered, they were taught sign language. That is the one case on record that seems to show that it doesn't take much in the way of stimulation to induce mental development of a natural language. Many interesting questions arise that could be settled with direct experiment, but these are of course excluded on ethical grounds, so more indirect approaches have to be taken.

QUESTION: Is the language acquisition device single or multiple? Can it be used once again in second and foreign languages? How about language acquisition in later life?

CHOMSKY: This comes back to the question that was asked before. It is probably true to say that in India or just about anywhere in the world, except parts of Western Europe, the United States, Japan, and a few other places, people often know lots of different languages. In most of human history, and in most parts of the world today, children grow up speaking a variety of languages. For example, if you grow up in West Africa, your mother may speak one language and your father another language and they may talk to each other in a third language and your aunt speaks a fourth language and so on without any known limit. That is just a natural state of human beings. In fact in an area like the United States where the native population was mostly eliminated and you have settlers coming in from mostly one place originally, you get an artificial sense of homogeneity; but that is just for historical reasons.

However, even in the United States, the idea that people speak one language is certainly not true. Everyone grows up hearing many different languages. Sometimes they are called 'dialects' or 'stylistic variants' or whatever, but they are really different languages. It is just that they are so close to each other that we don't bother calling them different languages. So everyone grows up in a multilingual environment. Sometimes the multilingual environment involves systems so unlike each other that you call them different languages. But that is just a question of degree; it is not a question of yes or no. So we know that whatever the language faculty is, it can assume many different states in parallel and we do not know how many different states. Children seem to be able to acquire quite a number of radically different languages without effort and without even awareness. Sometimes they don't even know, until they are four or five years old, that they are speaking different languages. That just seems to be a normal part of growth.

In any case, that is a more complicated question. The simpler question is how it works in a uniform situation. Only when that is more or less understood can one hope to investigate seriously the harder question: how it works in a *non*-uniform situation. The simpler one is hard enough.

How about language acquisition in later life, like if I wanted to learn, say, Hindi now? That is a different story. The reason is that there apparently is a critical period for language acquisition as in the case of most other bio-logical functions, perhaps several such periods. Take the visual system. You don't do experiments with humans, but people do experiments with cats or monkeys. So, if you prevent a monkey from getting patterned visual stimula-tion for more than a couple of weeks after birth, the visual system simply deteriorates. It has to have patterned stimulation at that point, or it is not going to function. In the case of a human, you have to have enough stimula-tion to get binocular vision by about four months, or else you'll never get it. Every biological property that is known has a period in which it has to be activated; after that period the capacity to activate it declines very sharply, or it may even disappear.

Language is probably like that too. It is easier to know in the case of the visual system and the reason is that we allow ourselves to torture cats and monkeys. So people do experiments with cats and monkeys and if you do experiments, you can get many answers very fast. Doctors used to but nowadays, at least in theory, we do not torture humans. You don't do the proper experiments with humans, thankfully. That makes it much harder to get the answers. We have to figure out indirect ways of getting them. But there is enough indirect evidence to suggest that there is a cut-off point to the ability to acquire language around age six or seven or eight (around there) and probably another cut-off around puberty. Those two changes, whatever they are, considerably restrict the capacity to acquire a second language. When you've passed a certain stage, you can acquire it but usually as a sort of growth on the language that you already have. Sometimes that difference is pretty subtle. You have to do subtle experiments to show it but it seems correct. These are interesting and important questions but hard ones, and there is also a good deal of individual variation in late language acquisition, which is not well understood.

QUESTION: Is it possible to have bilingual or trilingual children out of mixed marriages?

CHOMSKY: It doesn't make any difference. These things are all totally independent. It is like asking: can you have long arms coming out of mixed marriages? Or an interest in Greek philosophy?

THEORY OF LANGUAGE

QUESTION: Could you elaborate on the cosmic ray theory discussed in the talk? How did the principles of language get inserted in the genetic material of the wandering ape?

CHOMSKY: By the cosmic ray theory, I think you are referring to a certain fairy tale about human evolution, offered to help clarify some questions, but not to be taken very seriously (like most others that are offered). Specifically, the theory that some time ago there were primates with pretty much our sensorimotor and conceptual-intentional systems, but no language faculty, and some natural event took place that brought about a mutation that installed a language faculty. Say, a cosmic ray shower; or something that took longer, like the processes that caused a bone of the reptilian jaw to migrate to the inner ear, where it is wonderfully designed for the use of language—apparently, something that has been going on for about 160 million years as a mechanical consequence of growth of the skull in early mammals, so recent work suggests. The fairy tale is one way to motivate informally the questions raised in the Minimalist Program.

How did the basic principles get into the genetic programme? Such questions go vastly beyond current understanding, not just for language, but even for much simpler biological systems.

QUESTION: Infinite use of finite means; doesn't it entail an inconsistency? Isn't the model of an infinite potential in a finite organ inherently inconsistent?

CHOMSKY: That was the problem until about a century ago. It did look like an inconsistency. One of the important discoveries of modern mathematics is that it isn't an inconsistency. There is a perfectly coherent sense to the notion of infinite use of finite means. That is what ended up being the theory of computability, recursive function theory and so on.[22] It is a big discovery of modern mathematics which clarified traditional ideas. There have been sort of intuitive ideas like this around but they really became clarified quite recently—not really until almost mid-century. So, yes, it looks like an inconsistency but it simply isn't. There's a very simple account of it that is not inconsistent. I can't go into it any further here.

QUESTION: What is an example of a principle in the principles and parameters approach?

CHOMSKY: The principle that I mentioned in the talk that uninterpretable features have to be eliminated before semantic representation (or else the thing is illegible) and that the only way in which things can be eliminated is by erasure under very narrow locality—that appears to be a universal principle; it has consequences all over the place. For example, this technical question we just asked,[23] it has consequences for that. It is true across constructions, and across languages, so it appears. If so, that is a principle. Other principles of locality are also principles.

Proposed principles also include those of X-bar theory, binding theory, the c-command condition on chains, Kayne's theory of 'unambiguous paths' and its development to Larsonian 'shell theories', Rizzi's 'relativized minimality', and on, and on. The literature is full of them, and they are constantly changing; properly.[24]

The study of language is an ancient one, dating back to classical India and Greece. But questions of the kind now being investigated were not imagined, and could not have been raised until very recently. And the system is of an order of complexity where one does not expect stable far-reaching principles, in any area of empirical enquiry. An additional problem in this case is that obvious experiments, which might answer many questions quickly, are barred on ethical grounds, so it is necessary to proceed in far more indirect ways than in the study of complex molecules or the visual system of the cat.

QUESTION: Are you saying language is 'mid-way' in its 'perfection' between natural and formal systems? Is this an upshot of its 'recentness', or the sophistication of what it does?

CHOMSKY: References to the 'perfection' of language have to do with some questions that have only recently entered the research agenda, and are still poorly understood, but I think empirically meaningful and possibly important. The questions arise on the basis of certain (fairly standard) empirical assumptions—basically, that there is a dedicated language faculty that 'interfaces' with other ('external') systems that use the information provided by the language faculty to perform various actions. These external systems can only access information presented in certain forms; to be usable, the language must provide information in the appropriate form. The external systems, then, impose 'legibility conditions' ('bare output conditions', BOCs)[25] on the language faculty, and we can ask how well designed it is to satisfy these conditions, to what extent are properties of the language faculty 'best solutions' to the BOCs alone, introducing no independent complexity or technical devices not required by these conditions on access? The questions are initially imprecise, but can be refined in various ways as discussed in recent literature, which also investigates empirical consequences of adopting versions of the general thesis that language approaches 'perfection' in this sense.

Formal systems are a different matter entirely. They are artefacts designed for one or another purpose, and are good or bad to the extent that they serve these purposes. I see no interesting basis for comparison to a biological system. There is also no issue of 'recentness'. The questions arise in the same way, however the language faculty reached something like its current nature.

QUESTION: The Minimalist Program has thrown up various expressions like 'converge', 'crash', 'merge', 'procrastinate', 'greed'; aren't these metaphorical expressions borrowed from your political thought?

CHOMSKY: If so, it is unknown to me. 'Converge' and 'crash' come from mathematics and the theory of computation, 'merge' is the simplest way I can think of saying that two things come together to make a bigger thing, 'procrastinate' is kind of a semi-joke to keep things picturesque and intelligible. Same with 'greed'. I don't think the choice of terms means anything.

QUESTION: Left-to-right ordering of syntactic constituents has been accorded a more central and integrated role in the Minimalist Program than earlier. Is it inherently central to the architecture of the language faculty or is it more of an interface-constraint imposed by the sensorimotor and conceptual-intentional ordering considerations?

CHOMSKY: This is an interesting research topic. My own feeling is that there is no left-to-right ordering. If you look at the structure of the generative system (the system that takes lexical items and puts them together into bigger ones, performs operations on them and ends up giving semantic representations), if you take a look at these operations all the way down to the interface of the conceptual-intentional systems, it seems to have no left-to-right ordering. In fact it may be that it has no ordering at all; it just has hierarchical relations.

On the other hand, the sound has a left-to-right ordering. My assumption is that, that is imposed by the sensorimotor systems. Our sensorimotor systems are limited; they are forced to produce things from left to right, through time. So, somewhere along the line, this unordered system which has only hierarchy (and no order), gets an order imposed on it in order to meet conditions of the sensorimotor interface.

Notice that they are by no means necessary. In fact there are other organisms around that don't have that property. Take dolphins which have huge brains relative to size, not unlike humans. Dolphins have a complicated communication system. It comes out of their noses (dolphins make all kinds of funny noises); partly it is kind of sonar (they have to know where they are, if they are running into something), but partly it is apparently communication. Some sub-species of dolphins apparently can do it simultaneously through both sides of their nose. That means they have a richer form of communication than we have; they can produce sounds in parallel—two-dimensional production. That is certainly feasible; then these sounds don't have left-to-right order. They have parallel outputs, maybe left to right within each but not all left to right. We don't have that; we have a single channel.

Incidentally, if you look at sign language, it doesn't have a single channel. It has multiple channels, but articulated language does have a single channel. That is a limitation of our sensorimotor apparatus and it forces things to be ordered. If we had the ability to communicate by telepathy, let's say (so that we didn't have to make sounds), there might be no word ordering in language at all. [Inaudible intervention from the audience] Oh, sure; that is absolutely true but that is a different question.

Remember that the generation of an expression is an abstract operation; it is not the same as the production of an expression—that is a totally different thing. When you produce an expression, of course, it is temporal because you begin at a certain point and then you do the next thing and you do the next thing. You may make all kinds of changes along the way, but that is not the same question. When you make changes you are just regenerating some new thing; but generation and production are completely different operations. They are obviously related in that the performance systems have to access the knowledge system; so they are of course related but they are different operations. To say that generation has no order is independent of the fact that production has an order because we do things through time. That is not under discussion.

The question is, is there order in the abstract expression that provides the information? I think the answer is 'no' except close to the point of sensorimotor interface. But these are research questions; you can't be dogmatic about them.[26]

QUESTION: The core configurations adopted in the Minimalist Program such as spec-head relationship, or local relations, cannot explain the inflectional morphology involved in Tibeto-Burman languages such as Mizo. In Mizo, in the sentence which could be rendered in English as 'John wants to see you', the matrix verb 'want' agrees with the matrix subject 'John' as well as with the object 'you' of the embedded clause 'to see you'. In this case, we cannot establish a spec-head relation between the Agr_o of the matrix clause and the object of the embedded clause. How would you account for these facts in UG?

CHOMSKY: Suppose someone were to say that a particular approach to language cannot explain the fact that in English, the verb agrees with a deeply embedded noun phrase, not its own subject, in such expressions as 'there are believed to have been several people in the room'.[27] We cannot tell whether the statement is true or false. First, we would have to investigate English with some care, and also to determine how the approach in question should be refined as understanding progresses. No one has any idea whether the Minimalist Program offers a way to account for an example selected at random from a language, English or Mizo.

This is not something special about language. Even in the hard sciences, little is understood beyond pretty simple systems, and one can only speculate as to how the theories proposed might accommodate a specific phenomena, or even whether they do. Can the laws of physics explain the fact that it is raining right now? The question can't sensibly be asked in that form, and when it is asked properly, there seem to be some rather surprising answers, according to recent work. Early in this century, no one could say with any confidence whether the physics of the day, by far the most advanced of any of the branches of science, could account for such elementary matters as the chemical bond (it couldn't). Today, no one says with any confidence whether the physics of today can account for some 90 per cent of the postulated matter of the universe. When we turn to the earlier stages of the hard sciences, the conclusion is even more dramatic.

Science isn't in the business of carrying out miracles: rather, of advancing understanding, no easy task, even for what seem on the surface (often wrongly) to be the simplest questions.

QUESTION: X-bat theory can handle simple sentences including interrogatives and passives. Please let me know what will be the representation of complex sentences like (i) 'If he comes then we will go to the cinema', (ii) 'Though he is poor, he is honest'.

CHOMSKY: It is easy enough to propose phrase structure representations for expressions, though whether they should be in terms of X-bar theory is another question; personally, I'm sceptical, for reasons discussed in the recent minimalist work.[28] The question is which ones are correct, and that is no easier to answer for simple expressions than complex ones. Take 'you saw him', about as simple as you can get. Since the late eighties, it has been rather widely assumed that the phrase structure is quite different from what had been assumed earlier, perhaps something like:[29]

$$[_{IP}[_{DP} \text{ you } [_{I'} \text{ INFL } [_{VP} \text{ you } [_{V'} \text{ see } [_{DP} \text{ him}]]]]]]$$

Here the pair indicated informally as <you, you> is a 'chain' constructed by (perhaps rather complex) operations, which raise the lower occurrence of 'you' to the higher position, where it is heard. Similar question arise about the sentences you mentioned, which raise no special difficulties for phrase structure representation. There is interesting literature on these structures, for example, an MIT doctoral dissertation by Sabine Iatridou a few years ago.

QUESTION: What is the therapeutic value of the Minimalist Program?

CHOMSKY: Well, that was kind of a joke. What I said in chapter four of the book (Chomsky 1995b) was that even if the Minimalist Program doesn't work out, it has a therapeutic value. The value is that it forces you to think about things which you took for granted. If you were using X-bar theory or s-structures or indices or proper government, this programme forces you to ask the question whether these assumptions are really justified or whether you're just making them to cover up lack of understanding. That is therapeutic; it forces you to think about things that are easy to ignore.

For those of you in the discipline, if you look at the technical work in the field—let's say the attempts to explain the 'that'-trace-filter, you quite commonly discover that the proposals that are offered as explanations are of about the same order of complexity as the phenomena to be explained. They are not explanations; they're just restatements of the problem in other terms,[30] perhaps very useful in setting the stage for further work. The therapeutic value of this approach is that it digs that fact out and you get to see when you have an authentic explanation, and when you have something that you might be misleading yourself into thinking, is an explanation. There are a lot of such cases. For example, a lot of uses of such devices as proper government and indices turn out to be pseudo-explanations which restate the phenomena in other technical terms, but leave them as unexplained as before.

[Here's another example.] A guiding intuition of the programme is that operations apply anywhere. If so, then why do some operations, for example NP-movement, apply before spell-out and some after spell-out? This is pretty technical. With regard to NP-movement, there seems to be a crucial difference. Here's a new discovery, probably true. In very recent years, there's work coming along which suggests that . . . let me go back a step. There's good reason by now to assume that the noun-phrases in a sentence are all VP-internal, or, more generally, predicate-internal. Let's assume that.

A more recent empirical discovery is that in a verb phrase that involves expression of action (like a transitive verb or anything that has a causative or an agentive character, any such verb phrase) something has to escape visibly (that is, something has to appear outside), something has to be kind of thematized. The thing that can be thematized can be a subject going to specifier of tense or it can be an object (in languages that allow object-shift) going to the object-raising position of the verb phrase; but something has to be extracted, it seems. That means that, in a VSO language, the subject has actually gone to the specifier of tense position and it is a VSO language because of some superficial fact about the V moving even higher. So it means that there aren't any VSO languages really; there's just SVO languages or SOV languages.

It also means that if you have, say, a transitive-expletive construction in a language like Icelandic where it looks as if all the arguments are inside the verb phrase, at least one of them has escaped (it is not inside the verb phrase); at least one of them has moved, maybe the object.

That just looks like a fact and it is interesting to try to explain. It also seems to be a fact that the specifier of tense position has to be filled overtly. That is what is called the Extended Projection Principle; it looks like a universal descriptive property of language, probably associated with the same property of thematization. Those two facts force one case of NP-movement if the language doesn't have an expletive that can fill the subject position and if it is an agentive expression. So that looks forced by the universal principles of language.

What about other cases of NP-movement? For example, take a language like English that doesn't have overt object-raising like, say, Icelandic. It turns out that there is pretty good reason to think that English does have object-raising and it is even overt; but if it takes place, it has to be followed by another movement. So the object cannot stay in that position. That means that in a sentence like, 'What did John see?', the object first moves to the object-raising position just like in Icelandic or Japanese, but then it has to go on another step to the specifier-CP relation and that is for completely universal reasons plus a parametric difference having to do with properties of tense—it is a property that enters into Holmberg's generalization,[31] I think. So, there we have a parametric difference, a property of tense that yields Holmberg's generalization and that is going to make it look as if some languages have overt movement and others don't; but they all have. Now that combination of phenomena seems to determine if NP-movement appears before spell-out or not. It sounds like a complicated array of phenomena but if you think it through it is a very small number of things and the apparent differences seem very small.

QUESTION: What are the formal constraints imposed on a language by legibility requirements?

CHOMSKY: This is a research topic, and an evolving one. Even the study of conditions imposed by the sensorimotor systems, which have been investigated extensively for many years, is hard and complicated, with interesting but limited results. We know much less about the other systems of language use (those involved in thinking about the world, expressing our thoughts, asking questions etc.—sometimes called 'conceptual-intentional systems'). This research topic co-evolves with the study of the language faculty itself. I should stress that though understanding of systems external to the language faculty remains limited, there is a vast amount of relevant information about the conditions they impose—in fact, the information about sound and meaning that has always been used by the study of language, from its origins.

It is also worthwhile to recall that (relative) clarity is not a preliminary to research; rather an outcome. The questions that are asked become clearer as understanding of the answers deepens. There are myriad examples in the core natural sciences, right to the present.

QUESTION: What are the latest trends in semantics? Is it likely to develop into a science some day with its own units?

CHOMSKY: That is a really interesting question. That goes into one of those side issues about representations that I put aside in the talk. We have to ask what semantics is. If semantics is what is meant by the tradition (say, Peirce or Frege or somebody like that), that is, if semantics is the relation between sound and thing, it may not exist.[32]

If semantics is the study of relations like agency, thematization, tense, event-structures and the place of arguments in them and so on and so forth, that is a rich subject but that is syntax; that is, it is all part of mental representations. It goes on independently of whether there is a world at all just like the study of phonological representations. This is mislabelled 'semantics'. It would be like taking phonology and deluding yourself into thinking that phonology is the study of the relation between phonetic units and the motion of molecules; it isn't, that is a separate study. Phonology is the study of mental representations that one assumes are close to those parts of the processing system that ultimately moves molecules around. Most of what's called 'semantics' is, in my opinion, syntax. It is the part of syntax that is presumably close to the interface system that involves the use of language. So there is that part of syntax and there certainly is pragmatics in some general sense of what you do with words and so on.[33] But whether there is semantics in the more technical sense is an open question. I don't think there's any reason to believe that there is.

I think it goes back to the old and probably false assumption that there is a relation between words and things independently of circumstances of use.

QUESTION: By virtue of knowing the concept *climb*, does the child know that the concept needs an agent and a theme for its realization? Does the child learn that the concept of *die* is alternatively realized in English as 'die' and 'kick the bucket'? The innate conceptual and computational components are presumably different modules; does linguistic experience trigger some kind of interaction between them with the result that a predicate-argument structure is generated which is then converted into familiar lexically-filled syntactic representation?

CHOMSKY: These questions may be referring to a book of mine of about ten years ago in which I said that the child has a repertoire of concepts as part of its biological endowment and simply has to learn that a particular concept is realized in a particular way in the language.[34] So the child has a concept, say, *climb* in some abstract sense with all its weird properties and has to learn that it is pronounced 'climb', not some other thing. Jerry Fodor's important work for many years is relevant here, along with Ray Jackendoff's and much else.[35] These are all perfectly reasonable questions. You can have various ideas about them; there isn't a lot of understanding. I could tell you what my own suspicion is about these questions but they are research topics.

There is overwhelming reason to believe that concepts like, say, *climb, chase, run, tree* and *book* and so on are fundamentally fixed. They have extremely complex properties when you look at them. This is not recognized in traditional lexicography. When you read the huge *Oxford English Dictionary* (the one you read with a magnifying glass), you may think that you are getting the definition of a word but you're not. All you are getting is a few hints and then your innate knowledge is filling in all the details and you end up knowing what the word means. As soon as you try to spell out what's taken for granted in the lexicon, you find that these concepts are incredibly complex.[36]

Actually that was understood a couple of hundred years ago. There is a tradition roughly from Hobbes through Hume which investigated questions like these with some sophistication. I think it was the tradition which should be expanded; it had Aristotelian origins in fact and interesting parallels to seventeenth-century neo-Platonism.[37] But when you work these things out, it turns out that the concepts are very complex, which means that they've got to basically be there and then they get kind of triggered and you find out what sounds are associated with them.

But then come these questions: how much of this is variable? How much is fixed? Is the agent-theme property fixed or is it variable? That is a research topic. In some of the cases we know; for example, for 'die' and 'kick the bucket' obviously that is just artificially imposed. But for the other questions one doesn't really know.

Are the computational and conceptual components different modules? Really, that is not known very well either. That is the traditional question: can you have thought without language? If you ask how much we know about that topic, the answer is 'not much'. What we know is by introspection.

Now what seems to me obvious by introspection is that I can think without language. In fact, very often, I seem to be thinking and finding it hard to articulate what I am thinking. It is a very common experience at least for me and I suppose for everybody to try to express something, to say it and to realize that is not what I meant and then to try to say it some other way and maybe come closer to what you meant; then somebody helps you out and you say it in yet another way. That is a fairly common experience and it is pretty hard to make sense of that experience without assuming that you think without language. You think and then you try to find a way to articulate what you think and sometimes you can't do it at all; you just can't explain to somebody what you think. Sometimes you make judgements about things very fast, unconsciously. If somebody asks you how you made the judgement, it is often extremely hard to explain. Experiences like that seem to indicate that we can and do think without language and, if you are thinking, then presumably there's some kind of conceptual structure there. The question of how this is related to language is just another research topic which, at this point, can barely be touched; but it is potentially important and interesting.

NOTES

[1] See Pinker (1995) for a delightful account of current work on language.

[2] See Chomsky (1951).

[3] See Matthews (1964).

[4] See Jackendoff and Lerdahl (1983); also Jackendoff (1992).

[5] See Bernstein (1976).

[6] In Japanese, there is a sense of 'fly' in which people fly. In Hebrew, airplanes 'glide' but do not 'fly'.

[7] See the discussion on 'semantics' towards the end of 'Theory of Language'.

[8] Elsewhere Chomsky says the following about Jacques Laćan: In the case of Laćan, for example—it is going to sound unkind—my frank opinion is that he was a conscious charlatan, and was simply playing games with the Paris intellectual community to see how much absurdity he could produce and still be taken seriously. I mean that quite literally. I knew him (cited in Rai 1995: 206).

[9] See the first response in the next section, p. 50.

[10] See Stewart (1995) for a popular survey of this issue. See Penrose (1994) for similar examples and for related issues surrounding the theory of mind.

[11] See Hurford (1987) for a discussion of language and numbers.

[12] See Premack (1986) on these and related issues; also Pinker (1995), chapter 11.

[13] See Lieberman (1975) for an early classic discussion of the evolutionary bases of human speech. See Pinker (1995: chapter 11) for a review of more recent material from a different point of view.

[14] See Fodor (1975) for a classic statement of this hypothesis.

[15] The questioner probably has the analogy of the wandering ape, discussed in the talk, in *Mind*.

[16] See Chomsky (1980, chapter 6) for a lucid exposition of the notion of language faculty as an organ.

[17] For a popular survey of these issues, see Gardner (1975).

[18] See Hubel and Weisel (1962).

[19] See Curtiss (1977) for the full story.

[20] See Gleitman & Newport (1995); also, Carol Chomsky (1986).

[21] An ergative-absolutive language is one in which the subject of an intransitive verb and the object of a transitive verb have the same case-inflection. For an account of this in Minimalist terms, see Chomsky (1995b, chapter 3.2).

[22] See Turing (1950); also Boolos and Jeffrey (1974).

[23] See the discussion near the end of the talk on movement for feature-checking (for example, erasure of case-feature of nouns).

[24] See Radford (1988, 1997) for an introduction to these (highly technical) idea which can only be understood after a fair amount of work. Chapter 1 of Chomsky (1995b) also contains brief descriptions of them.

[25] See note 16 of Language and its Design.

[26] At this point, there is some mention of Richard Kayne's important work on linear ordering in syntax (Kayne 1994). Unfortunately, this part of the tape is largely inaudible. See Chomsky (1995b: 4.8) for a discussion of Kayne's theory.

[27] Notice that this construction, and the one of Mizo under reference, pose essentially the same problem: both appear to be instances of agreement between entities of different clauses, and, as such, appear to be counter-examples to the accepted idea that agreement is a clause-internal relation (in fact, a local specifier-head relation). The point is that what appears to be a counter-example on the face of it may not turn out to be so on closer and more careful analysis. For details regarding the so-called 'introductory "there"-constructions', see Chomsky (1995a, 1995b).

[28] See Chomsky (1995a).

[29] This representation is in terms of 'VP-internal subject hypothesis' (see Koopman and Sportiche 1991). The subject (i.e. the Determiner Phrase (DP)) originates in the Specifier position of VP—Spec of VP, and raises to the Specifier position of the Inflectional Phrase (IP)—Spec of IP, leaving behind a copy in the position of origin. Informally speaking, IP and DP and more recent notations for the familiar concepts S(entence) and Noun Phrase (NP), respectively.

In one earlier formulation, the phrase structure of the sentence under consideration is as follows:

$$[_{IP} [_{NP} \text{ you } [_{I'} \text{ INFL } [_{VP} [_{V'} \text{ see } [_{NP} \text{ him}]]]]]]$$

[30] ' "That"-trace' filter was proposed in Chomsky and Lasnik (1977) to account for the ungrammaticality of constructions such as *'Who do you think that saw Mary?', *'John seems that saw Mary'. In terms of the trace theory of movement, 'who' in the first example and 'John' in the second move from the subject positions of the respective subordinate clauses, leaving behind a trace. In each case, a ' "that"-trace' sequence is created. Compare the first example with 'Who do you think saw Mary?', which is grammatical. In the grammatical case, the complementizer 'that' does not occur, and as such the construction does not contain a ' "that"-trace' sequence. ' "That"-trace' filter evaluates as ungrammatical a construction that contains a ' "that"-trace' sequence. This filter is essentially a stipulation and is, in Chomsky's view, no more than a mere statement of the relevant phenomenon in a different form. For a more general account of the phenomenon, see Chomsky (1981, 1995b).

[31] See Holmberg (1986); see Chomsky (1995b:352-3) and Kitahara (1997) for some analysis.

[32] Elsewhere Chomsky makes a succinct observation in the same vein:

People use words to refer to things in complex ways, reflecting interests and circumstances, but *words* do not refer; there is no word-thing relation of the Fregean variety, nor a more complex word-thing-person relation of the kind proposed by Charles Sanders Peirce in equally classic work in the foundation of semantics. These approaches may be quite appropriate for the study of invented symbolic systems (for which they were initially designed at least in the case of Frege). But they do not seem to provide appropriate concepts for the study of natural language. (Chomsky 1996: 22-3)

[33] At this level there are issues concerning how one uses words to refer to things in the world and how one uses sentences to express attitudes and purposes: for one instance, the sentence

'drinks will be served at five' can be used as 'a promise, a prediction, a warning, a threat, a statement, or an invitation' (Chomsky 1975: 65), among others. See note above.

[34] See Chomsky (1988).

[35] See Fodor (1987), Jackendoff (1990).

[36] See Jackendoff (1990) for more on this.

[37] See Chomsky (1966, 1975, 1995c, 1997) for remarks on this tradition.

References

Barbosa, Pillar et al. (1998): *Is the Best Good Enough: Optimality and Computation in Syntax*, MIT Press, Cambridge.

Barsky, Robert (1997): *A Life of Dissent*, MIT Press, Cambridge.

Bernstein, Leonard (1976): *The Unanswered Question*, Harvard University Press, Cambridge.

Boolos, G. and R. Jeffrey (1974): *Computability and Logic*, Cambridge University Press, London.

Bresnan, Joan ed. (1982): *The Mental Representation of Grammatical Relations*, MIT Press, Cambridge.

Brody, Michael (1995): *Lexico-Logical Form: A Radically Minimalist Theory*, MIT Press, Cambridge.

Chomsky, Carol (1986): 'Analytic Study of the Tadoma Method: Language Abilities of Three Deaf-Blind Children', *Journal of Speech and Hearing Research*, September, pp. 332–47.

Chomsky, Noam (1951): *Morphophonemics of Modern Hebrew*, M.A. Thesis, University of Pennsylvania, published under the same title in 1979, Garland Press, New York.

———— (1955): *The Logical Structure of Linguistic Theory*, University of Pennsylvania. Most of the 1956 revision was published under the same title in 1975, Plenum Press, New York.

———— (1957): *Syntactic Structures*, Mouton, The Hague.

———— (1965): *Aspects of the Theory of Syntax*, MIT Press, Cambridge.

———— (1966): *Cartesian Linguistics*, Harper & Row, New York.

Chomsky, Noam (1972a): *Language and Mind*, expanded edition, Harcourt Brace Jovanovich, New York. Originally published in 1968.

———— (1972b): 'Remarks on Nominalization', in *Studies in Semantics and Generative Grammar*, Mouton, The Hague.

———— (1975): *Reflections on Language*, Pantheon Press, New York.

———— (1980): *Rules and Representations*, Basil Blackwell, London.

———— (1981): *Lectures on Government and Binding*, Foris, Dordrecht.

———— (1982): *Some Concepts and Consequences of the Theory of Government and Binding*, MIT Press, Cambridge.

———— (1986a): *Knowledge of Language*, Praeger, New York.

———— (1986b): *Barriers*, MIT Press, Cambridge, Mass.

———— (1987a): *Generative Grammar: Its Basis, Development and Prospects*, Kyoto University of Foreign Studies, Kyoto.

———— (1987b): *Language in a Psychological Setting*, Sophia University, Tokyo.

———— (1988): *Language and Problems of Knowledge*, The Managua Lectures, MIT Press, Cambridge.

———— (1991): 'Linguistics and Adjacent Fields', in Asa Kasher, ed., *The Chomskyan Turn*, Basil Blackwell, Oxford.

———— (1993a): *Language and Thought*, Anshen Transdisciplinary Lecture, Moyer Bell, London.

———— (1993b): 'Mental Construction and Social Reality', in E. Reuland and W. Abraham, eds, *Knowledge and Language*, Kluwer Academic Publishers, Dordrecht.

———— (1994): 'Naturalism and Dualism in the Study of Language and Mind', Agnes Cuming Lecture (1993), *International Journal of Philosophical Studies*, Vol. 1.

———— (1995a): 'Bare Phrase Structures', in H. Campos and P. Kempchinsky, eds, *Evolution and Revolution in Linguistic Theory*, Georgetown University Press, Washington.

———— (1995b): *The Minimalist Program*, MIT Press, Cambridge.

———— (1995c): 'Language and Nature', *Mind*, January, pp 1-61.

Chomsky, Noam (1996): *Powers and Prospects: Reflections on Human Nature and Social Order*, Madhyam Books, Delhi.

——. (1997): 'Language and Mind: Current Thoughts on Ancient Problems', Parts 1 and 2 (mimeograph).

——. (1999): 'Mininalist Inquiries: The Teamwork', *Step by Step: Minimalist Papers in Honor of Howard Lasnik*, MIT Press, Cambridge.

Chomsky, N., R. Huybregts and H. Reimsdijk (1982): *The Generative Enterprise*, Foris Publications, Dordrecht.

Chomsky, N. and H. Lasnik (1977): 'Filters and Control', *Linguistic Inquiry*, 8, pp. 425–504.

Curtiss, Susan (1977): *Genie: A Psycholinguistic Study of a Modern-Day 'Wild-child'*, Academic Press, New York.

Fodor, Jerry (1975): *The Language of Thought*, Crowell, New York.

—— (1987): *Psychosemantics*, MIT Press, Cambridge.

Gardner, Howard (1975): *The Shattered Mind*, Alfred Knopf, New York.

Gazdar, Gerald, E. Klein, G. Pullum and I. Sag (1985): *Generalised Phrase Structure Grammar*, Basil Blackwell, Oxford.

George, Alexander (1987): 'Review of *Knowledge of Language*', *Mind and Language*, Vol. 2, No. 2, pp. 155–64.

Gleitman, L. and E. Newport (1995): 'The Invention of Language by Children: Environmental and Biological Influences on the Acquisition of Language', in Daniel Osherson, ed., *An Invitation to Cognitive Science*, Vol. 1 (edited by Lila Gleitman and Mark Liberman), MIT Press, Cambridge.

Holmberg, Anders (1986): *Word Order and Syntactic Features in the Scandinavian Languages and English*, Doctoral Dissertation, University of Stockholm.

Hurford, James R. (1987): *Language and Numbers: The Emergence of a Cognitive System*, Basil Blackwell, Oxford.

Hubel, D. and T. Weisel (1962): 'Receptive Fields, Binocular Vision and Functional Architecture in the Cat's Visual Cortex', *Journal of Physiology*, 160, pp. 106–54.

Iatridou, Sabine (1991): *Topics in Conditional*, Ph.D. Dissertation, MIT.

Jackendoff, Ray (1990): *Semantic Structures*, MIT Press, Cambridge.

—— (1992): *Languages of the Mind*, MIT Press, Cambridge.

Jackendoff, R. and F. Lerdahl (1983): *A Generative Theory of Tonal Music*, MIT Press, Cambridge.

Katz, Jerold and Jerry Fodor, eds (1964): *The Structure of Language*, Prentice-Hall, Englewood Cliffs.

Kayne, Richard (1994): *The Antisymmetry of Syntax*, MIT Press, Cambridge.

Kitahara, Hisatsugu (1997): *Elementary Operations and Optimal Derivations*, MIT Press, Cambridge.

Koopman, H. and D. Sportiche (1991): 'The Position of Subjects', in J. McClosky, ed., *The Syntax of Verb-initial Languages*, Elsevier, North-Holland.

Lasnik, Howard and M. Saito (1984): 'On the Nature of Proper Government', *Linguistic Enquiry*, 15, pp. 235–89.

Lee. R. B. (1957): 'Review of the Syntactic Structures by Chomsky, N.', in *Language*, Vol. 33–3, pp. 375–405.

Lieberman, Philip (1975): *On the Origins of Language*, Macmillan, New York.

Mathews, G. H. (1964): *Hidatsa Syntax*, Mouton, The Hague.

Otero, Carlos, ed. (1994): *Noam Chomsky: Critical Assessments*, Vol. 1, Routledge & Kegan Paul, London, p. 342.

Penrose, Roger (1994): *The Shadows of Mind: A Search for the Missing Science of Consciousness*, Oxford University Press, Oxford.

Piattelli-Palmarini, Massimo, ed. (1980): *Language and Learning: The Debate between Jean Piaget and Noam Chomsky*, Harvard University Press, Cambridge.

Pinker, Steven (1995): *The Language Instinct*, HarperCollins, New York.

Premack, David (1986): *Gavagai: Or the Future History of the Animal Language Controversy*, MIT Press, Cambridge.

Radford, Andrew (1988): *Transformational Grammar*, Cambridge University Press, London.

———— (1997): *Introduction to Minimalist Syntax*, Cambridge University Press, London.

Rai, Milan (1995): *Chomsky's Politics*, Verso, New York.

Stewart, Ian (1995): *Nature's Numbers: Discovering Order and Pattern in the Universe*, Weidenfeld and Nicolson, London.

Turing, Alan (1950): 'Computing Machinery and Artificial Intelligence', *Mind*, July.

Wexler, Ken (1991): 'On the Argument from the Poverty of the Stimulus', in Asa Kasher, ed., *The Chomskyan Turn*, Basil Blackwell, Oxford.

Zubizarreta, Maria L. (1998): *Prosody, Focus and Word Order*, MIT Press, Cambridge.

Index